# Increasing Student Achievement through High-Performance Teacher Leadership

# Increasing Student Achievement through High-Performance Teacher Leadership

Matthew J. Jennings

ROWMAN & LITTLEFIELD
*Lanham • Boulder • New York • London*

Published by Rowman & Littlefield
An imprint of The Rowman & Littlefield Publishing Group, Inc.
4501 Forbes Boulevard, Suite 200, Lanham, Maryland 20706
www.rowman.com

86–90 Paul Street, London EC2A 4NE, United Kingdom

Copyright © 2022 by Matthew J. Jennings

*All rights reserved.* No part of this book may be reproduced in any form or by any electronic or mechanical means, including information storage and retrieval systems, without written permission from the publisher, except by a reviewer who may quote passages in a review.

British Library Cataloguing in Publication Information Available

**Library of Congress Cataloging-in-Publication Data**

Names: Jennings, Matthew, author.
Title: Increasing student achievement through high-performance teacher leadership / Matthew J. Jennings.
Description: Lanham, Maryland : Rowman & Littlefield Publishing Group, 2022. | Includes bibliographical references. | Summary: "This book proceeds to provide a method for selecting teacher leaders, identification of a realistic set of performance expectations and a means for comprehensively and systematically evaluating job performance"—Provided by publisher.
Identifiers: LCCN 2021037556 (print) | LCCN 2021037557 (ebook) | ISBN 9781475863260 (cloth) | ISBN 9781475863277 (paperback) | ISBN 9781475863284 (epub)
Subjects: LCSH: Educational leadership. | Teachers—In-service training. | Teachers—Rating of. | Academic achievement.
Classification: LCC LB2806 .J47 2022 (print) | LCC LB2806 (ebook) | DDC 371.2/011—dc23
LC record available at https://lccn.loc.gov/2021037556
LC ebook record available at https://lccn.loc.gov/2021037557

# Contents

Acknowledgments vii

1 Introduction 1
2 Creating Conditions that Support Teacher Leadership 23
3 Collaborative and Interpersonal Skill Development 45
4 Mapping the Terrain: "School Politics and Culture" 65
5 Promoting Professional Growth 81
6 Instructional Leadership 97
7 Human Resources Management 115

Bibliography 123

About the Author 127

# Acknowledgments

I want to thank my wife, MaryAnn Jennings, for her help with the formatting of this text. I would also like to thank my daughter, Tara Jennings, for her proofreading and revision suggestions. Without the help from each of you, this book would not have reached the level of quality desired.

*Chapter 1*

# Introduction

Imagine a meeting held in the principal's conference room. Seated around the table are three teachers, the principal, and the assistant principal. Each teacher in turn provides an update on the status of their current activities. The first teacher shares plans for an upcoming series of after-school workshops. She is pleased with the number of staff that have expressed interest and plan to attend. In addition, she is confident in her preparation and is optimistic that the sessions will have a positive impact on the work of her colleagues.

The next teacher shares the result of his recent data analysis meetings with the grade-level teams. He is satisfied with the type and level of analysis conducted but is concerned with some identified gaps in the curriculum. He shares a proposal for curriculum revision that is well received by the rest of the group. The assistant principal offers his assistance in arranging the time for staff to complete this task.

The third teacher informs the rest of the group about recent mentoring activities. Her report focuses on the activities conducted during the previous month between mentors and mentees. In her recent meeting with the mentors, she was informed that many of the mentees are confused by the district's grading policy. She shares her plan for working with the mentor teachers to rectify these misunderstandings. The principal offers to reach out to the district assistant superintendent for clarification on a few of the most confusing remaining items.

The group concludes the meeting with a discussion on the responsibilities for an upcoming recruiting trip to a local college. Collaboratively they decide who will conduct screening interviews for potential candidates. The meeting concludes with setting a date for conducting comprehensive interviews of selected candidates for the two positions that are open for the subsequent school year.

This type and level of teacher-administrator collaboration is possible. Given clearly defined responsibilities and supportive conditions, the right teachers can have a significant and positive impact on a school's instructional program. Through their actions, these teachers can improve their colleagues' work, which in turn will improve student achievement. However, none of this is possible without a clear vision and mission for teacher leadership.

**Vision and Mission.** What is teacher leadership? If a random group of educators was asked this question, it is very likely the responses would vary widely. However, efforts to initiate or refine teacher leadership must begin with clarity of the vision and mission for why and how this strategy will be implemented. The vision for teacher leadership articulated in this book is one in which *competent, credible, collaborative faculty members use specialized knowledge and skills to influence one or more aspects of the school or district's instructional program.*

Teacher leadership is a means to an end. To be successful, teacher leadership initiatives require a clearly established purpose. The purpose of the teacher leadership described in this book is for *administrators and teacher leaders to share expertise and use collaborative decision-making as they demonstrate collective responsibility for ensuring the school-wide instructional excellence needed for achieving significant student learning gains.* Ultimately, the mission of teacher leadership is increased student achievement.

To achieve this vision and mission as it is described earlier, it is critical for those with responsibility for planning and implementation to adhere to a set of core beliefs about teacher leadership. The following list of beliefs is a concise summary of the key points made in subsequent chapters.

## BELIEFS ABOUT TEACHER LEADERSHIP

- Roles and responsibilities for teacher leaders vary based upon available resources and site-specific needs.
- The roles and responsibilities of teacher leaders must be clear to administrators and staff. Furthermore, these roles and responsibilities must focus on improving instruction, staff collaboration, and, ultimately, student achievement.
- Effective teacher leaders maintain a role as part-time classroom instructors.
- The selection process for teacher leaders must be fair, transparent, and include faculty input.
- Teacher leadership is neither for everyone nor is it possible for all teachers at various life stages.
- The development of teacher leadership is a long-term commitment by the school and district.

- School administrators must establish the conditions necessary for teacher leaders' success.
- The cultural norms of a school play a significant role in the potential effectiveness of teacher leaders.
- Teacher leaders and school principals need one another to succeed if they are to maximize their effectiveness.
- Teacher leaders need adequate time for preparation and collaboration.
- Teacher leadership consists of a set of skills that can be learned.
- Teacher leaders require high-quality professional learning designed to provide them with the knowledge and skills necessary to perform their assigned roles and responsibilities.
- Strong communication and interpersonal skills are essential to the success of all teacher leaders regardless of assigned roles and responsibilities.
- Teacher leaders need ongoing support from administrators, mentors, and colleagues in order to continue learning and growing.
- The achievements of teacher leaders need to be recognized.
- The work of teacher leaders must be evaluated based on clear performance standards with an emphasis on reflection and growth.
- Teacher leaders are accountable for producing mutually agreed-upon results.

Each of these belief statements will be further explained in subsequent chapters, but first, it is important to consider the potential benefits of teacher leadership.

**Benefits of Teacher Leadership.** Unlike classroom teaching, teacher leadership does not have a direct impact on improving student achievement. It is a mediating factor with the ability to positively influence variables that do have direct impacts on student learning and achievement. More specifically, teacher leadership opportunities can increase teacher job satisfaction resulting in higher teacher retention rates. In addition, distributing aspects of instructional leadership to teacher leaders can result in increased faculty collaboration as well as meaningful changes to instructional practices.

**Teacher Retention and Job Satisfaction.** According to the National Center for Education Statistics (2016), 8 percent of teachers leave the profession yearly and another 8 percent move to other schools, bringing the total annual turnover rate to 16 percent. Thus, on average, a school will lose three out of every twenty teachers yearly. Less than a third of national teacher attrition is due to retirement (Carver-Thomas & Darling-Hammond, 2017). Therefore, each year schools nationwide must hire tens of thousands of teachers as a result of beginning and mid-career teachers leaving the profession.

High teacher attrition has several harmful effects. First, high turnover rates create extra costs for schools. It has been estimated that the cost to replace one teacher in an urban school district is $20,000 (Carver-Thomas & Darling-Hammond, 2017). Second, research shows that teacher attrition reduces student achievement. Specifically, high teacher turnover results in lower student scores in both English Language Arts (ELA) and math (Ronfeldt et al., 2012). Lastly, teacher turnover harms school operations by disrupting school stability and results in a loss of vital institutional knowledge.

One factor cited by ex-teachers for why they chose to leave the profession is a lack of influence on school decision-making (Carver-Thomas & Darling-Hammond, 2017). Teachers deprived of the ability to make decisions on what they perceive as critical issues report greater dissatisfaction with their job, more stress, and less loyalty to their principal (Levin & Shrum, 2017). Through appropriately structured leadership opportunities, teachers will have the voice they desire in decisions related to classroom practice.

Appropriately involving teacher leaders in shared decision-making is not only important for job satisfaction but may also lead to better-quality decisions. Teacher leaders who have regular classroom interactions with students and peers are in an excellent position to make informed decisions about issues related to teaching and learning. Whether it is textbook selection, curriculum revision, or the development of common formative assessments, teacher leaders have the direct exposure needed to know what has the highest probability of success.

As an added benefit, those who meaningfully participate in decision-making demonstrate more commitment to follow through on the actions required as a result of those decisions. In addition, when teacher leaders participate in both shaping and leading change initiatives, resistance from faculty is greatly decreased (Katzenmyer & Moller, 2009). Teacher leaders are uniquely positioned to get buy-in for reforms that education officials, even principals, cannot (Margolis, 2009).

A second factor cited by ex-teachers for leaving the profession is the lack of opportunity for career advancement (Carver-Thomas & Darling-Hammond, 2017). In most professions, the more knowledge and expertise one gains, the more responsibility one assumes. This is not the case in teaching, where the twenty-year veteran's responsibilities are essentially the same as the newly licensed novice's.

The MetLife Survey of the American Teacher (2020) found that 51 percent of all teachers are at least somewhat interested in teaching in the classroom part-time, combined with other roles and responsibilities. This same survey found that only 16 percent of teachers were interested in becoming a school principal.

Research conducted by Harvard University's Project on the Next Generation of Teachers found that unlike their predecessors, many beginning teachers have a strong interest in differentiated hybrid roles that would allow them to continue teaching while moving beyond the classroom to have a greater influence in schools (Peske et al., 2001).

Thus, a significant percentage of teachers want to assume leadership responsibilities without directly relinquishing all direct instructional responsibilities. Appropriately structured teacher leadership opportunities will make this goal possible and therefore will result in greater rates of teacher retention over time.

**Instructional Leadership.** Effective instructional leadership has been linked to improved instruction and enhanced student outcomes (Goddard et al., 2015). Despite its importance, it appears that the demands placed on school leaders make it very difficult for them to adequately serve in this capacity. In fact, researchers have found that school leaders are typically only able to focus on instructional leadership tasks for between 8 and 17 percent of their working hours (Horng et al., 2010; Grissom et al., 2013).

Considering the importance of instructional leadership and school leaders' inability to provide it, educators must find ways to share this responsibility. Providing trained teacher leaders with instructional leadership responsibilities is a sensible solution. In fact, teacher leadership in aspects of instruction may lead to improved student achievement.

Using survey and test score data across sixteen states, Ingersoll and colleagues (2017) examined the relationship between teacher instructional leadership and school performance. These researchers concluded that schools with the highest levels of overall instructional leadership from teachers had substantially higher math and ELA test scores in their state compared to those where teachers report low levels of leadership in these areas.

In some situations, teacher leaders may have a more substantial impact on faculty instructional practices than school administrators. A teacher who knows another teacher that had success with a new approach is more likely to adopt a similar new practice (Katzenmyer & Moller, 2009). As experienced, effective teachers, teacher leaders are "in the trenches." Thus, teacher leaders' suggestions are perceived as "more legitimate" than those that do not teach.

**Collaboration.** Teachers improve their practice at greater rates when they work in schools with higher-quality collaboration (Ronfeldt et al., 2015). In fact, teachers working in schools with strong, professional working environments are much more likely to improve over several years than peers in schools with weak environments (Kraft & Papay, 2016). Teacher leadership opportunities provide one way to increase collaboration and communication between school staff members (Wilson, 2016; Beachum & Denith, 2004).

In particular, Ronfeldt and colleagues (2015) found that joint work on student assessments was often a significant predictor of student achievement gains in math and reading. Additionally, Papay and colleagues (2016) found that when higher- and lower-performing teachers were encouraged to scrutinize each other's evaluation results, observe each other teaching in the classroom, discuss strategies for improvement, and follow up with each other's commitments throughout the year, higher student scores on assessments of reading and math were the result. In sum, teacher collaboration matters for improving student learning. In addition, collaboration also has a positive impact on teachers' professional learning.

Williams (2014) found that teachers learn best from colleagues and supervisors who help them take risks and embrace their weaknesses. Additionally, in studies of teachers who use formative assessments to boost student learning, he found that teachers improve their teaching most when they serve as resources for one another and develop a sense of ownership for their professional development.

Thus, it is reasonable to conclude that the most powerful professional learning tends to be shared among colleagues, not vested in one person who is high up in the hierarchy (York-Barr & Duke, 2004). Teacher leaders fill this role by making professional learning a socially distributed phenomenon that develops over time, among faculty members.

Lastly, administrative turnover frequently results at the end of initiatives. As one administrator leaves, the initiatives they started come to an end, only to be replaced by initiatives brought forth by the new administrator. The result is a sequence of partially implemented school-improvement efforts. This is both ineffective and frustrating for those teachers left behind.

Teacher leaders can usually be counted on to remain in their schools through administrative turnover. As a result, they can provide the continuity needed to sustain initiatives. Teacher leaders provide an approach to building and sustaining organizational capacity, thus increasing the possibility for successful reforms.

Of course, none of the positive impacts described in this section will occur if teacher- leader roles and responsibilities are either poorly defined or consist primarily of low-impact activities. In fact, if the most effective classroom teachers are filling teacher leadership roles, than the low-impact teacher leadership roles that take them away from providing instruction can actually be detrimental to student achievement.

**Roles and Responsibilities.** Teacher leader roles and responsibilities are seldom well-defined. Uncertainty about teacher leader versus principal domains of leadership can contribute to conflict. In addition, lack of clarity regarding roles, responsibilities, and authority can create distrust with peers. To be effective, teacher leaders must have clear and explicit responsibilities. Furthermore, these responsibilities must be articulated to all of the adults working with teacher leaders.

In order to be effective for peers and students as well as motivating for teacher leaders, the focus of responsibilities must be on the improvement of instructional practices across the learning organization. Engagement of teacher leaders in valued instructional work is considered a key factor in their success (York-Barr & Duke, 2004). In addition, remaining responsible for some classroom teaching is important for teacher leaders.

Teacher leaders that devote part of their time to classroom teaching keep their teaching skills fresh and stay connected to student and peer needs and challenges. In addition, dual structures allay other teachers' concerns about the creation of status differentials and the formation of a new oligarchy among teachers (Murphy, 2005).

When deciding upon roles and responsibilities for teacher leaders, it is important to remain cognizant of the fact that the more ambitious the conception of teacher leadership, the more likely it is to spark conflict. For this reason, it is wise to start focused and let additional leadership responsibilities evolve over time (Carr et al., 2005). However, this gradual approach must not be miscommunicated as lack of long-term commitment to teacher leadership.

Teachers know that leadership positions funded by temporary grants or political line items are tenuous. As a result, it may be difficult to recruit the right candidates and the position may not be taken seriously. The following is a sample job description for teacher leadership positions. This description must be revised to fit the needs and context of each school district.

## JOB DESCRIPTION: TEACHER LEADER

### Relationship Within School System

The teacher leader reports to the school principal.

### Major Functions

Teacher leaders use specialized knowledge and skills to influence one or more aspects of the school or district's instructional program with the intention of improving student learning. The specific focus of teacher leaders may vary depending on agreed-upon needs in individual school buildings. Summative evaluations will reflect this fact.

### Principal Duties and Responsibilities

*Domain 1—Interpersonal and Communication Skills*

Teacher leaders use effective interpersonal and communication strategies to build relationships, communicate information, and help groups accomplish tasks. Examples of responsibilities demonstrating performance of this standard include but are not limited to

- building and maintaining positive interpersonal relationships with support staff, colleagues, and administrators;
- utilizing oral and written communication skills to provide information in a clear, concise, and timely manner;
- utilizing active listening skills to build trust, create understanding, and clarify meaning;
- utilizing conflict resolution strategies to resolve issues while preserving relationships and valuing a diversity of opinions;
- utilizing problem-solving and decision-making strategies to generate, evaluate, and select alternative choices;
- utilizing knowledge of group development and meeting facilitation skills to efficiently accomplish group tasks.

## Domain 2—*Professional Learning and Growth*

Teacher leaders use knowledge of the characteristics of adult learners and change management strategies to promote the professional learning of colleagues. Examples of responsibilities demonstrating performance of this standard include but are not limited to

- demonstrating knowledge of the characteristics of adult learners;
- designing, delivering, and evaluating professional learning activities;
- utilizing knowledge of change management to positively influence the capacity of others to implement initiatives.

## Domain 3—*Instructional Leadership*

Teacher leaders use data, coaching skills, and curriculum knowledge to promote continuous improvement of instruction. Examples of responsibilities demonstrating performance of this standard include but are not limited to

- accessing, collecting, organizing, and analyzing data in order to identify goals and measure progress;
- utilizing a structured approach to coaching classroom instruction, including providing constructive and descriptive feedback designed to enhance teaching practices;
- facilitating the review and revision of school and/or district curriculum documents.

## Domain 4—Human Resources Management

Teacher leaders use organizational skills, professional judgment, and communication skills to assist with the recruitment, selection, orientation, and mentoring of new staff members. Examples of responsibilities demonstrating performance of this standard include but are not limited to

- assisting with the planning, organizing, implementing, and evaluating of the new teacher orientation and mentoring program;
- organizing the placement of student teachers and interns, in order to facilitate the achievement of a positive and productive experience;
- participating in the process of interviewing potential employment candidates;
- representing the school and/or district at job fairs.

## Domain 5—School Community and Advocacy

Teacher leaders understand and ethically use knowledge of school culture and politics to positively influence school climate and achieve desired outcomes. Examples of responsibilities demonstrating performance of this standard include but are not limited to

- demonstrating an understanding of school culture;
- using influence strategies to shape school culture so it is conducive to student learning;
- demonstrating an understanding of school and district politics;
- ethically using knowledge of school and district politics to accomplish tasks.

## Domain 6—Professionalism

Teacher leaders maintain a professional demeanor, participate in professional growth opportunities, and contribute to the profession. Examples of responsibilities demonstrating performance of this standard include but are not limited to

- remaining aware of current research regarding the best practices in curriculum and instruction;
- contributing to the profession through presentations at local, regional, state, or national conferences;
- contributing to the profession through publication in scholarly journals;
- serving on committees of professional organizations;
- completing applications for grant funding.

*Domain 7—Student/Program Progress*

The work of the teacher leader results in acceptable, measurable student and/or program progress based on established personal, school, and/or district goals. Examples of responsibilities demonstrating performance of this standard include but are not limited to

- achieving school goals as dictated by the annual school-improvement plan;
- achieving approved annual student/program goals.

## Evaluation

Performance of the responsibilities associated with this position will be evaluated using the Teacher Leader Summative Evaluation Form.

## Standards of Eligibility

1. Department of Education Standard Instructional Certification.
2. Summative evaluation ratings of effective or higher for the past three years.

## Preferred Qualifications

1. Demonstrated ability to develop positive and trusting relationships with staff members.
2. Exemplary listening skills.
3. History of commitment to ongoing professional development and self-reflection.
4. Proven interest in the improvement of peers' instructional practices.
5. Understanding of how to use data and educational research.
6. History of supporting and strengthening the school community.
7. Demonstrated history of appropriate advocacy for the needs of staff and students.

## Length of Work Year and Compensation

1. Based on the annual school calendar.
2. Annual compensation rate determined by the Negotiated Agreement.

Crafting and then providing a job description such as this establishes the qualifications and responsibilities for the position. The established qualifications and responsibilities should serve as the framework for conducting a fair selection process.

**Teacher Leader Selection Process.** The goal of the selection process is to choose the most qualified candidate(s) using a process that is perceived as fair and transparent. If the teacher leader selection process is perceived as unfair and/or lacking in transparency, it may contribute to conflict and undermine the potential effectiveness of those selected for the position.

Similarly, administrators whom select teacher leaders without teacher input risk being perceived as demonstrating favoritism. Teacher leaders selected because of perceived favoritism will lack support from colleagues (Danielson, 2006). Thus, it is prudent to form a committee of representative stakeholders to complete the selection process.

In addition, leadership roles must not be determined based solely on seniority. Selecting teachers solely based on years of experience results in the appointment of teacher leaders that may or may not possess the required skills. Furthermore, teachers should not be "voluntold" to be teacher leaders.

There are times when a teacher may be eager to pursue teacher leadership and other times when that same teacher may retreat from these responsibilities. Reluctance to take on leadership roles may stem from a desire to protect the time needed to balance work and personal responsibilities. The reality of struggles and demands with personal issues may mean that teachers are compelled to move in and out of leadership roles.

Additionally, not all teachers are interested in leadership roles. Teaching well and engaging in ongoing professional improvement can be a life-long endeavor. Teachers who choose not to assume formal teacher-leader roles are no less professional than those who do. Rather, they have chosen to focus their energies on refining their craft within their own classroom instead of extending beyond it. In sum, selecting the wrong candidates for the wrong reasons undermines the credibility and the potential effectiveness of the entire endeavor.

The process of hiring teacher leaders is an attempt to determine two subjective indicators of "fit." First, the committee attempts to estimate the level of job fit. In other words, committee members evaluate whether an applicant possesses the qualifications that meet the job requirements. Second, the committee attempts to determine the level of person-to-organization fit. Does the applicant have the personality, values, and interests that correspond to the school's organizational values and culture? The major vehicle used to make these determinations of "fit" is interviews. Any interview process can result in a wide range of outcomes, ranging from a very high to a very low ability to predict the success of job candidates. In other words, poorly designed and conducted interviews will provide very little insight into the applicants' potential to perform in the organization. On the other hand, even though the best selection methods will sometimes lead to bad hiring decisions, in the long run more valid methods will dramatically increase the proportion of good hiring decisions.

Research clearly suggests that hiring decisions based on intuition or "gut feelings" are likely to be suboptimal, even when performed by seasoned interviewers (Roulin, 2017). Used with fidelity, a structured interview protocol will increase the probability that a committee will make a better hiring decision.

**Protocol Development.** Decades of employment interview research have highlighted the value of structured interviews. More specifically, interviews in which the questions are prepared in advance, all interviewees are asked the same questions in the same order, and anchored rating scales are used to score and compare applicants' responses lead to better hiring decisions. This type of systematic, standardized approach reduces the risk of biases, errors, and personal preferences.

Of course, the types of questions asked matter. The questions used must accurately capture the job requirements of the teacher leader. To achieve this goal, the questions developed for this protocol are based on the responsibilities specified in the previously provided job description. The committee may decide to weigh specific questions based on current needs, but this decision must be made in advance of the interviews.

The best predictor of future behavior is past behavior. In other words, if someone was able to use specific knowledge, skills, or abilities to achieve something in the past, they are very likely to be able to replicate the same behavior again in the future when facing a similar situation. Thus, all of the questions asked are phrased to gather information about the application of specific skills to solve particular job-related problems.

To evaluate the applicants' responses, anchored rating scales and sample indicators of performance have been provided. The sample indicators provide characteristics and examples of what might be included in a high-quality response. The sample indicators are not all inclusive and cannot be used as a checklist. The rating scales provide a systematic means for evaluating and comparing candidates' responses.

**Use of This Protocol.** The first step in using this protocol is a review of the candidate's credentials. The credentials included on this form are those associated with the preparation required to be a successful teacher leader. Using the Credential Review Form (figure 1.1) to analyze information provided by the candidates enables the committee to validly and fairly select the highest potential candidates for inclusion in the interview pool. The number of candidates selected for the initial screening interview will depend upon the quality of the recruiting pool and the breadth of candidates desired by the committee.

**Credential Review Form**

Applicant's Name  _____    _____
                           Last                                First

*CREDENTIAL QUALIFIERS*

| | |
|---|---|
| 1. **Education** – 3 points maximum<br>1 point = Master's Degree<br>3 points = Ph.D. or Ed.D. | |
| 2. **Experience** – 6 points maximum<br>1 point per year for full-time experience as a teacher<br>2 points per year for full-time experience working in a teacher leadership capacity | |
| 3. **Special Training** – 3 point maximum<br>1 point for each specialized training experience related to teacher leadership | |
| 4. **Contributions to the Education Profession** – 3 points maximum<br>1 point = organizes, facilitates, and/or presents at local, state and/or national conferences; maintains an active role in professional organizations; serves as an instructor, mentor, or coach<br>2 points = serves on local, state, or national committees; researches and publishes academic work | |
| **(Maximum score = 15)** | |

**Figure 1.1  Credential Review Form.**

At a minimum, two committee members should complete the Credential Review Form for each candidate. Upon completing their ratings, committee members can compare results. At this point, disagreements between two raters about a candidate's credentials can be resolved by the completion of a rating by a third person.

Once an initial interview pool is selected, the committee will schedule and conduct interviews. It is vitally important for the reliability and validity of the interview instrument that the questions are asked in the same order and in the same manner to all of the candidates. This is the purpose of the structured Comprehensive Teacher Leader Interview (figure 1.2).

It is not recommended that committee members probe candidates' responses. The reason for this is that it could potentially provide opportunities for candidates to share information other candidates did not have the opportunity to share, thus reducing the validity and fairness of the interview.

It could be acceptable to use a standard follow-up question for each candidate in an attempt to prompt a complete response. For example, if a candidate does not provide a connection between actions they have taken and the improvement of a school district, the interviewer can ask the follow-up question, "How did the actions you describe lead to improvements in a school district?"

**Applicant's Name:** _____

**Date:** _____  **Time:** _____

**Name of Interviewer:** _____

*Convert ratings into points and write the number of points in the blank beside the question number.*

*(Highly Effective = 4; Effective = 3; Partially Effective = 2; Ineffective = 1)*

*Then, add the numbers to get a subtotal for the Performance Quality. Finally, sum the subtotals to get an overall rating. The maximum score is 32 points.*

| Performance Quality | Question Prompts |
|---|---|
| Instructional Leadership | 1 ____ + 5 ____ = ____ |
| Interpersonal and Communication Skills | 2 ____ + 6 ____ = ____ |
| Professional Learning and Growth | 3 ____ + 7 ____ = ____ |
| School Community and Advocacy | 5 ____ + 8 ____ = ____ |

**Total Score for Candidate:** _____

Figure 1.2  Comprehensive Teacher Leader Interview.

Importantly, to ensure fairness and validity, this would need to be asked of every candidate, for every question in which the information was not provided.

Upon completing the interview questions, interviewers should use their notes to individually complete the rating scales and develop the overall score. If a candidate's answer has all of the elements of a lower category and some of the elements of a higher category, it is acceptable to assign a 0.5 score (i.e., 2.5 instead of 2.0 or 3.0). Candidates with the highest average overall scores will be tentatively selected for the position.

## Directions

*This interview contains eight question prompts interviewers can use to rate an applicant's responses during the interview. For each question, there are multiple prompt options. Select one prompt from each question to ask the applicant. Only ask one prompt option for each question.*

*Immediately after the applicant has responded, score the response by placing an "X" in the box next to the term that best describes the quality of the applicant's response.*

*At the conclusion of the interview, the ratings will be entered in the Overall Rating Total.*

# 1. INSTRUCTIONAL LEADERSHIP (PEDAGOGICAL AND CONTENT KNOWLEDGE)

## Prompt Options

- Please provide us with an example of a time when you shared your instructional or content knowledge to improve the performance of a colleague.
- Tell us about a time when you used your knowledge and experience with classroom management to help a colleague.
- Please share with us how you have used your knowledge of assessment to improve achievement results for students.

## Sample Quality Indicators

- Demonstrates knowledge of high-quality instruction
- Demonstrates knowledge of effective classroom management strategies
- Demonstrates knowledge of effective assessment practices

Table 1.1   Instructional Leadership (Pedagogical and Content Knowledge)

| ☐ Highly Effective 4 Points | ☐ Effective 3 Points | ☐ Partially Effective 2 Points | ☐ Ineffective 1 Point |
|---|---|---|---|
| The response demonstrates a sophisticated and extensive understanding of effective pedagogy. | The response demonstrates solid understanding of effective pedagogy. | The response demonstrates partial understanding of effective pedagogy. | The response does not demonstrate understanding of effective pedagogy. |

Notes:

# 2. INTERPERSONAL AND COMMUNICATION SKILLS (DEVELOPING POSITIVE AND TRUSTING RELATIONSHIPS)

## Prompt Options

- Please describe strategies you have used to develop positive and trusting relationships with your colleagues.

- Please tell us about a time when you provided constructive feedback to a staff member. Specifically, describe the content of the feedback, how you shared it, and how it was received.
- Tell us about a time when the viewpoint of a colleague changed your opinion on a school-related topic.

*Sample Quality Indicators*

- Develops positive and trusting relationships with staff
- Effectively provides feedback
- Values diverse opinions

Table 1.2 Interpersonal and Communication Skills (Developing Positive and Trusting Relationships)

| ☐ *Highly Effective* 4 Points | ☐ *Effective* 3 Points | ☐ *Partially Effective* 2 Points | ☐ *Ineffective* 1 Point |
|---|---|---|---|
| The response demonstrates a sophisticated and highly effective use of skills to develop positive and trusting relationships with staff members. | The response demonstrates effective use of skills to develop positive and trusting relationships with staff members. | The response demonstrates limited skill in developing positive and trusting relationships with staff members. | The response does not demonstrate skill in developing positive and trusting relationships with staff members. |

Notes:

## 3. PROFESSIONAL LEARNING AND GROWTH (COMMITMENT TO IMPROVEMENT OF PRACTICE)

### Prompt Options

- Provide an example of a recent professional learning activity you participated in. Specifically, what was the content, why did you participate, and how did you use what you learned?
- Describe a professional learning activity you voluntarily completed recently. What was the activity, why did you complete it, and how did you apply what you learned?

*Sample Quality Indicators*

- Continuously strives to improve professional practice
- Proactively participates in professional learning opportunities

Table 1.3  Professional Learning and Growth (Commitment to Improvement of Practice)

| ☐ *Highly Effective* 4 Points | ☐ *Effective* 3 Points | ☐ *Partially Effective* 2 Points | ☐ *Ineffective* 1 Point |
|---|---|---|---|
| The response demonstrates an exemplary commitment to the continuous improvement of professional practice resulting in effective implementation of new skills and knowledge. | The response demonstrates commitment to continuously improving professional practice with some evidence of implementation of new skills and knowledge. | The response demonstrates limited commitment to the improvement of professional practice. | The response does not demonstrate commitment to improvement of professional practice. |

Notes:

## 4. SCHOOL COMMUNITY AND ADVOCACY (SUPPORTING AND STRENGTHENING THE SCHOOL COMMUNITY)

## Prompt Options

- **Describe a school initiative you voluntarily participated in. Specifically, what was the initiative, what was your role, and why did you choose to participate?**
- **Provide an example of an action you have taken to improve school climate.**

*Sample Quality Indicators*

- Voluntarily participates in school initiatives
- Demonstrates commitment to improving school culture and climate

**Table 1.4  School Community and Advocacy (Supporting and Strengthening the School Community)**

| ☐ Highly Effective<br>4 Points | ☐ Effective<br>3 Points | ☐ Partially Effective<br>2 Points | ☐ Ineffective<br>1 Point |
|---|---|---|---|
| The response demonstrates an extensive commitment to proactively supporting and strengthening the school community.<br>Notes: | The response demonstrates commitment to supporting and strengthening the school community. | The response demonstrates limited commitment to supporting and strengthening the school community. | The response does not demonstrate commitment to supporting and strengthening the school community. |

## 5. INSTRUCTIONAL LEADERSHIP (UNDERSTANDING DATA AND RESEARCH)

### Prompt Options

- Share with us how you use student data to make instructional decisions.
- How have you recently used educational research to inform your pedagogical practices?

*Sample Quality Indicators*

- Understands effective use of student data
- Understands educational research
- Uses educational research to inform pedagogy

**Table 1.5  Instructional Leadership (Understanding Data and Research)**

| ☐ Highly Effective<br>4 Points | ☐ Effective<br>3 Points | ☐ Partially Effective<br>2 Points | ☐ Ineffective<br>1 Point |
|---|---|---|---|
| The applicant demonstrates the systematic and extensive use of student data and/or educational research to make instructional decisions.<br>Notes: | The response demonstrates an understanding of using student data and/or educational research for making instructional decisions. | The response demonstrates a partial understanding of using student data and/or educational research for making instructional decisions. | The response does not demonstrate an understanding of using student data and/or educational research for making instructional decisions. |

## 6. INTERPERSONAL AND COMMUNICATION SKILLS (ALTRUISM AND SENSITIVITY)

### Prompt Options

- Provide an example of an action you have taken that communicated to a colleague that you cared about their success.
- Tell us about a time when you demonstrated sensitivity to the thoughts and feelings of one or more colleagues.

### Sample Quality Indicators

- Expresses interest in others success and/or well-being
- Demonstrates sensitivity to the thoughts and feelings of others

Table 1.6   Interpersonal and Communication Skills (Altruism and Sensitivity)

| ☐ Highly Effective 4 Points | ☐ Effective 3 Points | ☐ Partially Effective 2 Points | ☐ Ineffective 1 Point |
|---|---|---|---|
| The response demonstrates a high level of commitment to the success of colleagues and/or high levels of empathy. Notes: | The response demonstrates altruistic behavior toward colleagues and/or sensitivity to their thoughts and feelings. | The response indicates limited altruistic behavior and/or sensitivity to the thoughts and feelings of others. | The response does not indicate altruistic behavior and/or sensitivity to the thoughts and feelings of others. |

## 7. PROFESSIONAL LEARNING AND GROWTH— (CONTINUOUS SELF-REFLECTION)

### Prompt Options

- **Provide an example of how you engage in self-reflection to improve your professional practice.**
- **Describe a situation when you reached out to a colleague or supervisor for feedback on an idea or problem.**

### Sample Quality Indicators

- Actively engages in ongoing self-reflection
- Seeks feedback
- Willingness to admit not knowing something

Table 1.7  Professional Learning and Growth – (Continuous self-reflection)

| ☐ Highly Effective<br>4 Points | ☐ Effective<br>3 Points | ☐ Partially Effective<br>2 Points | ☐ Ineffective<br>1 Point |
|---|---|---|---|
| The response demonstrates the sophisticated and extensive use of self-reflection to improve professional practice. | The response demonstrates continuous use of self-reflection to improve professional practice. | The response demonstrates limited use of self-reflection to improve professional practice. | The response does not demonstrate the use of self-reflection to improve professional practice. |

Notes:

## 8. SCHOOL COMMUNITY AND ADVOCACY (ADVOCACY)

### Prompt Options

- **Provide an example of how you have demonstrated advocacy for the school and/or school district.**
- **Tell us about a time when you advocated for the needs of staff and/or students at your school. Specifically, what did you advocate for and why?**

*Sample Quality Indicators*

- Advocates appropriately for the needs of staff and students
- Speaks positively about the school and district

Table 1.8  School Community and Advocacy (Advocacy)

| ☐ Highly Effective<br>4 Points | ☐ Effective<br>3 Points | ☐ Partially Effective<br>2 Points | ☐ Ineffective<br>1 Point |
|---|---|---|---|
| The response demonstrates the sophisticated and extensive use of advocacy skills to address the needs of staff and students. | The response demonstrates the ability to effectively advocate for the needs of staff and students. | The response demonstrates limited attempts to advocate for the needs of staff and students. | The response does not demonstrate advocacy for the needs of staff and students. |

Notes:

Conclude the interview by doing the following:

- Asking the applicant if there is anything else about his or her professional background he or she would like for you to know.
- Asking the applicant if he or she has any questions.
- Letting the applicant know when he or she is likely to hear from the committee again.
- Thanking the applicant for his or her time.

The final step in this interview protocol is checking an applicant's references via a phone interview. Of course, this is not required if the individual is a well-known internal candidate. The Reference Check Form (figure 1.3) asks references to evaluate the applicant's previous performance in the same major categories as the interview protocol questions.

This information can be used to confirm the information provided by the candidate during the interview process. In other words, the applicant's

---

Applicant Name: _____

Date of Reference Check: _____  Person Checking Reference: _____

Reference Name: _____  Reference Organization: _____

Relationship to Applicant: ____ Supervisor  ____ Peer  ____ Other (Specify)

Position(s) Held: _____  Reason for Separation: ____
Voluntary ____ Involuntary ____

*Explain to the reference that the purpose of this call is to determine if this candidate would be a good fit to lead the (insert name) school district.*

Compared to other people you have managed or worked with, how does this candidate compare in:

| | | | | | |
|---|---|---|---|---|---|
| Developing positive and trusting relationships | Poor | Fair | Good | Very Good | Excellent | N/A |
| Commitment to the improvement of instruction | Poor | Fair | Good | Very Good | Excellent | N/A |
| Altruism and sensitivity | Poor | Fair | Good | Very Good | Excellent | N/A |
| Self-reflection | Poor | Fair | Good | Very Good | Excellent | N/A |
| Pedagogical and content knowledge | Poor | Fair | Good | Very Good | Excellent | N/A |
| Understanding data and research | Poor | Fair | Good | Very Good | Excellent | N/A |
| Supporting and strengthening the school community | Poor | Fair | Good | Very Good | Excellent | N/A |
| Advocacy for the school | Poor | Fair | Good | Very Good | Excellent | N/A |

**Purpose:** A reference check is a valuable tool in the recruitment process used to verify facts and obtain additional information about the candidate. To be considered a valid reference, all sections must be completed. Indicate N/A if the question is not applicable. *DO NOT CONDUCT A CHECK WITHOUT PERMISSION FROM THE CANDIDATE.*

If asked, what would others in your organization say about this candidate?
*Thank the reference for their time and willingness to share their opinion*

**Figure 1.3  Telephone Reference Check Form.**

average rating by the interview committee should be similar to the ratings provided by the aggregate responses of the references. If this is not the case, additional information should be sought and caution should be taken prior to making a final interview decision.

In this chapter, teacher leadership has been defined and the rationale for supporting its use has been established. In addition, a means for articulating job qualifications and responsibilities has been provided as a process for selecting candidates. Regardless of how qualified the candidates selected may be, their ultimate effectiveness will depend upon having supportive working conditions. Creating supportive working conditions for teacher leaders is the subject of chapter 2.

*Chapter 2*

# Creating Conditions that Support Teacher Leadership

The content of chapter 1 identified potential roles, responsibilities, and qualifications for teacher leadership positions. Additionally, the process for a fair and transparent selection process was described. Implementation of this content will help teacher leaders succeed, but it is not enough. Teacher leadership will only thrive if the school culture and school administration are supportive, if adequate collaboration time and professional development are provided, and if incentives, recognition, and evaluation serve as motivators for those that accept the role.

## SCHOOL CULTURE

A school's culture is a complex pattern of norms, attitudes, beliefs, behaviors, values, ceremonies, traditions, and myths that are deeply ingrained in the very core of the organization (Barth, 2002). Culture is a historically transmitted pattern of meaning that wields tremendous power over what people think and how they act. Some school cultures are hospitable to reform and innovation, whereas others are a barrier.

In the case of teacher leadership, the culture determines to a large degree the extent to which teachers will be able to acquire and exercise leadership skills (Danielson, 2006). If the cultural norms promote teacher leadership, then teacher leadership is far more likely to be a positive and productive influence on school achievement. However, far too often this is not the case.

Teaching is not a profession that values or encourages leadership within its ranks (Murphy, 2005). In fact, leading from within the ranks is, in many ways, a countercultural act. Teacher leadership is a countercultural act because the teaching profession is characterized by norms of egalitarianism, autonomy, and seniority.

The egalitarian norms of school cultures suggest that all teachers should be equals. Because teacher leadership creates a hierarchy within the faculty, it violates this norm. As a result, in school cultures with strong egalitarian norms, those that assume teacher leadership positions are viewed as "stepping out of line" or crossing over to side with administration.

Two significant problems related to teacher leadership result from this egalitarian norm. First, fearing the reactions of colleagues, teachers will hesitate to assume leadership positions. Second, those that do assume leadership positions can be expected to be punished by fellow teachers (Barth, 2013). According to Murphy (2005), teachers are often not gentle with colleagues who violate egalitarian norms. Obviously, neither of these outcomes are beneficial for the implementation and growth of teacher leadership.

Norms associated with seniority equate status and privilege with longevity. In other words, teachers that have been teaching for an extended period of time within a school should be treated with deference and respect by colleagues. According to this norm, first choice in opportunities should be provided to those with seniority, and their input on decisions should be given extra credence. The obvious problem with this norm is the fact that longevity does not always equate with expertise or effectiveness.

Thus, in a school culture that values seniority, a teacher with less experience who is more effective in promoting student achievement will not be granted the same level of respect as those with more years in the classroom. Regardless of knowledge or skill, the less experienced teacher will lack the credibility required to be perceived as worthy of teacher leadership. As a result, less experienced but more effective teachers may not apply for teacher leadership positions and those that do will face the obstacle of perceived illegitimacy.

The traditional norm pervasive in many schools is that teaching is a private practice. A teacher is expected to be responsible for his or her own students in his or her own classroom. Teachers should not interfere in another's classroom affairs as to do so is to suggest criticism. In addition, this norm implies that teachers with more than a few years of experience should be self-reliant. In essence, where this norm is pervasive teachers may be congenial toward one another, but there is no genuine collegiality.

By its very nature, teacher leadership requires collaboration. Teacher leadership thrives in a culture characterized by a shared sense of responsibility for the learning of every student. If teacher leaders are to have a meaningful impact, then school cultures must eliminate the current "egg-crate" structure that reinforces classroom boundaries.

All school cultures are incredibly resistant to change (Barth, 2002). Yet, if changes are made to a school's organizational structure without addressing impeding aspects of the school's culture, innovations such as teacher leadership are not likely to take hold. Administrators considering providing teacher leadership opportunities must examine the current school culture in order to assess the viability of this strategy.

If the school culture is characterized by norms of egalitarianism, seniority, and autonomy, then the culture must be changed to replace these norms with ones characteristic of collegiality and professionalism. Inserting teacher leaders into an unsupportive culture is setting them up to fail. In addition to the culture of the school, successful teacher leadership depends on the support of school administrators.

## SCHOOL ADMINISTRATION

The relationship between teacher leaders and their principals is consistently identified as having a strong influence on teacher leadership (York-Barr & Duke, 2004). Without principals who value teacher leadership and demonstrate willingness to shift their own beliefs, roles, and responsibilities, it is highly unlikely teacher leadership can succeed.

One aspect of teacher leadership influenced by the principal-teacher relationship is that of teachers' interest in applying for the role. Teachers' initial willingness to assume leadership roles is highly dependent upon having a positive and respectful relationship with their principal (Murphy, 2005). Teachers do not seek opportunities to lead with principals they do not feel valued by and/or do not respect.

Even though the role of principal support is clear, there is evidence to suggest that it is more readily espoused than enacted (York-Barr & Duke, 2004). Successful teacher leadership requires principals to give up power, and some principals are reluctant to cede what they consider their authority.

While the sharing of power by the principal is critical to the success of teacher leadership, it does come with risk and sacrifice. It can be difficult for principals to relinquish power when they continue to retain the ultimate responsibility and accountability for school outcomes. For this risk to be taken willingly, principals must value the expertise of teacher leaders and acknowledge that they can contribute to solving substantive and complex challenges.

Another aspect of the principal-teacher leader relationship that must be considered is the provision of meaningful leadership opportunities. For teacher leadership to be successful, the principal must provide teacher leaders with significant and authentic leadership opportunities in areas that utilize their talents and expertise. Principals must build teacher leadership roles into the structure of their schools so that teacher leaders can actively engage in partnership with school administrators.

In addition to sharing power and providing meaningful leadership opportunities, principals must serve as advocates for teacher leadership. Advocacy begins with explaining to the faculty the roles and responsibilities of teacher leaders. Faculty must understand the potential advantages of teacher leadership as well the type of authority or influence teacher leaders will have. When providing this explanation, the principal must choose his or her words carefully. Any suggestions of teacher leaders having administrative authority should be avoided at all costs.

In addition, it is important for the principal to periodically share with the rest of the staff what teacher leaders are accomplishing when they are not in the classroom. While this information can be shared in a variety of ways, the most important point is to focus on what teacher leaders are doing to improve teaching and learning.

Whereas principals must demonstrate willingness to share power, provide meaningful leadership opportunities, and advocate for teacher leadership, teacher leaders must also do their part to make this relationship productive. More specifically, teacher leaders must demonstrate that they are trustworthy, able to acknowledge the "big picture," and support the vision and goals of the administration.

Trust is the foundation of a productive working relationship. To build and maintain a trusting relationship requires teacher leaders to consistently and repeatedly demonstrate specific behaviors. First, teacher leaders must demonstrate the ability to maintain confidentiality. Teacher leaders are likely to become privy to information that is not available to the rest of the faculty. The principal must know that the information shared with teacher leaders will not be disclosed to others.

Second, teacher leaders must demonstrate the ability to keep their commitments. Assigned tasks must be completed at the level of quality expected and on time. At a minimum, if it is not possible to complete the task, the teacher leader must inform the principal as soon as possible of the reasons for the situation.

Third, teacher leaders must never cover up mistakes. For building and maintaining trust, admitting mistakes and taking the appropriate actions to remediate the situation is far superior to hoping those mistakes will not be discovered.

Lastly, teacher leaders cannot withhold important information from their principal. Allowing the principal to be blindsided when it could be prevented is certain to have long-lasting, damaging effects on trust.

In sum, a positive and productive working relationship cannot be developed without sufficient levels of interpersonal trust. Also necessary for a positive and productive relationship between teacher leaders and principals is the ability to acknowledge understanding of events at a more global level.

Teachers can be quick to criticize administrators for not taking actions they believe to be the best. Teachers may accuse principals directly or otherwise of being weak, unsupportive leaders. However, there are times when teachers do not have a comprehensive understanding of the situation beyond the four walls of their classrooms. As a result, teachers may not understand the ramifications of the actions they seek.

In addition, just as teachers sometimes receive a mandate they don't necessarily agree with but must follow, principals sometimes encounter the same situation. One difference is that the principal may not have the ability to express his or her disagreement or even acknowledge the source of the directive. Trusting that the principal is acting in the best interest of the school as a whole, teacher leaders acknowledge that there are reasons for the principal's actions they may not understand.

The final area of the relationship the teacher leader must attend to is being supportive of the principal. Teacher leaders must avoid showing up their principal and must never publicly criticize or disagree with them. Of course, when teacher leaders disagree with the principal's actions, they should have the opportunity to voice their concerns privately and appropriately. However, even if they disagree with it, once a decision is made the teacher leader must publicly support it. Doing so presents the faculty with the unified front required to build confidence in school leadership.

## TIME

Time for collaboration and completion of teacher leadership responsibilities are repeatedly cited as barriers to effective teacher leadership (Phelps, 2008). Teacher leaders require sufficient, predictable, and dedicated release time to fulfill their responsibilities. Without this time, teacher leadership responsibilities will become an add-on to the teacher's current responsibilities, resulting in the depletion of time and energy.

Optimally, teacher leaders will spend between 40 percent and 60 percent of their work time teaching, with the remainder of their time dedicated to teacher leadership responsibilities. The amount of time required will depend upon the actual responsibilities assigned to the teacher leaders. In general, the more time dedicated to teacher leadership activities, the higher the expectations for substantial responsibilities can be.

In situations where dedicated time is not built into the schedule, it must be carved out from otherwise scheduled activities. At a minimum, teacher leaders typically need common planning time, substitute coverage for peer observation, and use of faculty meeting time for professional development. When less time is available for exercising teacher leadership activities, expectations for substantial responsibilities must be adjusted accordingly.

## INCENTIVES AND RECOGNITION

Teachers who assume formal leadership roles deserve compensation that is commensurate with the responsibilities of those roles. If additional compensation for teacher leadership is provided, the amount will likely be negotiated with the local collective bargaining unit. Considering the factors involved in deciding the amount of additional pay, it is impossible to suggest a universally appropriate amount.

Unfortunately, most teacher-leader roles are low- or no-paying roles, and few pay adequately through recurring funding (Murphy, 2005). This fact sends a message about the importance of teacher leadership to school success. If professional work is regarded as important and teacher leaders are regarded as professional, then appropriate compensation should reflect this fact.

In addition, in many schools there is limited nonfinancial recognition for the work of teacher leaders. In fact, in far too many places the only reward for teacher leadership is added responsibility. There are two sources of nonfinancial recognition that can energize teacher leaders.

First, peer acceptance and recognition are highly valued. In healthy school cultures, all members respect, acknowledge, and celebrate one another's expertise and contributions to the organization, the profession, and the achievement of shared goals. Teacher leaders are motivated by feedback indicating they have made a significant, positive impact on their peers.

Second, the actions of persons of status and influence are important sources of recognition. Specifically, principals need to find ways to reward teacher leaders in ways that they value. Honoring requests for professional development or initiating opportunities for them to serve as representatives of the school at important meetings are examples of ways principals can show respect and appreciation for teacher leaders' work. Regardless of the form it takes, school leaders must provide meaningful incentives and rewards for teachers who take the lead in tackling tasks and solving problems.

## PROFESSIONAL DEVELOPMENT

Teachers enter the profession possessing few leadership skills (Murphy, 2005). Thus, without the appropriate preparation, teachers tapped for leadership roles are commonly unprepared. Creating leadership roles and then providing inadequate preparation for enacting these roles will lead to failure and disillusionment. It is irresponsible to significantly expand teachers' authority without preparing them to use it well.

Fortunately, leadership skills can be learned. All teacher leaders need opportunities to learn and develop communication and interpersonal skills. With their lack of formal authority, teacher leaders' ability to influence colleagues depends on their ability to establish and maintain positive working relationships. The content required for the development of these skills is the subject of chapter 4.

Additional content for the professional learning of teacher leaders should be tailored to the identified roles and responsibilities they will assume. For example, if they will be serving in the role of instructional coaches, then they will require training in observation skills and the provision of meaningful performance feedback. If they are not assigned this responsibility, then they do not require this training. Chapters 5 through 7 contain the content needed for fulfilling most of the professional responsibilities that will be assigned to teacher leaders.

As with the development of any complex skill set, the process for growing and developing as a teacher leader takes time. Acquisition of new knowledge and skill requires explicit instruction, practice applying the new knowledge, feedback from experts and colleagues, and ongoing support for maintaining the newly adopted practices. Growing teacher leaders is a process, not an event.

## EVALUATION

The formal evaluation of teacher leaders rarely aligns with their responsibilities (Murphy, 2005). In order for the results of the evaluation process to be meaningful for teacher leaders, there must be a clear set of performance standards; regular opportunities for reflection, feedback, and goal setting; and intermittent expert judgment of performance based on established transparent criteria.

The following manageable process meets these criteria and can thus be used to conduct an evaluation that is both valid and emphasizes reflection, leading to professional growth. The following teacher surveys provide formal opportunities for feedback from faculty members. The program growth objective process provides the opportunity for goal setting. A portfolio provides the opportunity for reflection. The summative evaluation provides the opportunity for expert judgment of performance. All of these tools are aligned to the domain standards stated in the job description presented in the first chapter.

Changes may be required based on local circumstances. However, keeping the job description responsibilities, the data collection tools, and the evaluation criteria aligned is important for establishing a fair process.

## TEACHER SURVEYS

When teacher leaders appropriately reflect upon and then use the feedback they receive from teacher surveys, it can lead to improvement in their performance. Teacher surveys focus on the means rather than the ends. As a result, they give teacher leaders tangible ideas about the changes they can make during the school year. The teacher survey questions used accurately reflect the teacher leader expectations articulated in the job description provided in chapter 1.

## TEACHER SURVEY DIRECTIONS

1. The teacher leader shall administer the same Teacher Survey (table 2.1) in October and March.
2. After the survey has been completed, the teacher leader shall compile the results and complete the appropriate self-reflection form (form 1 and form 2). The surveys themselves remain the property of the teacher leader.
3. The required self-reflection forms shall be included in the teacher leader's portfolio.

## TEACHER SURVEY—TEACHER LEADERSHIP

**Directions**: Please read the statements below. For each statement, place an X in the box that identifies your level of agreement with that statement. *Do not write your name on this survey.* When you have completed the survey, please return it to my mailbox. _____ is the deadline date for the return of the survey.

**Table 2.1  Teacher Survey – Teacher Leadership**

| Statement | Strongly Agree | Agree | Disagree | Strongly Disagree |
|---|---|---|---|---|
| The teacher leader develops trusting relationships with adults. | | | | |
| The teacher leader provides constructive and actionable feedback. | | | | |
| The teacher leader values diverse opinions. | | | | |
| The teacher leader expresses interest in peers. | | | | |
| The teacher leader shows sensitivity to peers. | | | | |
| The teacher leader runs effective meetings. | | | | |
| The teacher leader uses group processes (the processes people use to solve a problem or make a decision) effectively. | | | | |
| The teacher leader mediates diverse viewpoints. | | | | |
| The teacher leader facilitates professional learning that improves the practice of peers. | | | | |
| The teacher leader differentiates professional learning for adults at different skills levels. | | | | |
| The teacher leader facilitates conversations that prompt self-reflection. | | | | |
| The teacher leader helps others use data to make decisions. | | | | |

## TEACHER SURVEY SUMMARY (FORM 1)

Teacher Leader's Name: _____ School Year: _____

**Teacher Response Analysis**

1. How many surveys were distributed and how many were returned?

2. List any factors that might have influenced the responses:

3. What did teachers perceive as your strengths?

4. What did teachers perceive as areas in need of improvement?

5. What, if anything, do you need to do differently as a result of these responses?

## TEACHER SURVEY SUMMARY (FORM 2)

Teacher Leader's Name: _____ School Year: _____

**Teacher Response Analysis**

1. How many surveys were distributed and how many were returned?

2. List any factors that might have influenced the responses:

2. What did teachers perceive as your strengths?

3. What did teachers perceive as areas in need of improvement?

4. What, if anything, changed significantly since the first time you administered the survey?

**Program Growth Objective Form.** This Program Growth Objective Form (figure 2.1) is intended to provide teacher leaders with an annual improvement process they can use to both grow professionally and contribute to the overall quality of education provided in their school or district. The following template is intended to serve as the organizing structure for plan development and documentation.

When deciding on the focus for the plan, an early decision to make is whether the plan will be completed individually or as part of a team. Both of these choices have advantages and disadvantages. Completion of a team project provides opportunities for group problem-solving, shared opportunities for data analysis, and verification of results in multiple settings. On the other hand, a teacher leader may have a unique focus or face constraints that make collaboration difficult. Either way, at the start of the plan the teacher leader must decide and communicate if this will be a team plan and, if so, who the team members are. Communicating this decision will help the responsible administrator organize and coordinate the work of staff members.

**Identified Area for Growth.** There are four parts to be considered when identifying a selected area for growth. The first of these areas is the development of a S.M.A.R.T. goal. The content of this goal should be a high-priority area for student and/or teacher growth. This should be a data-driven decision based on student results from quality assessments.

The content of a S.M.A.R.T. goal is designed to answer the question: What do I (or we) seek to accomplish, with whom, by how much, and by when? S.M.A.R.T. is an acronym for the criteria to be used for developing effective goals. Each letter stands for:

*S*—*S*pecific—states exactly what you seek to accomplish.
*M*—*M*easurable—can be quantified.
*A*—*A*ttainable—can be achieved.
*R*—*R*elevant—important to you.
*T*—*T*ime Bound—timeframe for achieving the goal.

An example of a S.M.A.R.T. goal is: *By April 2021, improve third grade student performance by an average of 25 percent in number sense and operations as measured by district benchmark assessments.*

The S.M.A.R.T. goal must be connected to one or more change ideas. Each change idea is a strategy intended to be implemented in order to reach the identified goal. Similar to S.M.A.R.T. goals, change ideas must be focused, testable, measurable, and actionable within a reasonable timeframe. An example change idea is: *Three days per week, during the last five to ten minutes of math class, students will write reflections on what they learned. These reflections will be recorded in math journals with the prompts provided varying based on the content.*

Change ideas originate from three sources. First, teacher leaders can read research to determine what the literature says about solving the identified problem. Second, teacher leaders can ascertain what colleagues have done to solve similar problems. Last, teacher leaders can create original solutions to address the problem. The change idea may originate from one or any combination of these three sources.

The content of the evidence section of professional growth plan identifies the process or outcome measures to be used to determine if the change idea resulted in the desired improvement. For example, *student math journal entries will be assessed using a rubric. These rubric scores will be recorded and analyzed to determine if there is a correlation between improved rubric scores and increased performance in the areas of number sense and operations on district benchmark assessments.*

The final section of the area-for-growth portion of the template is the prediction. The content of this section identifies what the teacher leader believes will happen or hopes to see happen by implementing the change idea. The predictions need to be measurable and observable in order to determine whether they were met at the end of implementation of the plan. For example: *As a result of using math journals, students will*

1. *summarize important content,*
2. *identify connections between current and previously learned content, and*

3. *describe how the content will be used in the future.*

*Through achieving these actions students will have the opportunity to make sense of and find meaning in the content taught. This will result in increases in long-term retention of math learning.*

**Action Plan and Data Collection.** The action-plan section of the template is for identifying and sequencing the major steps of the implementation process. Each step shall include a deadline for completion. If the plan involves more than one person, then it is appropriate to decide and record individual responsibilities.

To determine the effectiveness of the change idea, the teacher leader must identify methods to assess progress. There are two general categories of measurements teacher leaders can use to reach this goal. Process measures are used to determine whether the successful implementation of a change idea is occurring before the final outcomes are known. These strategies are monitored formatively so that appropriate aspects of the change idea can be revised in a timely manner. The journal rubric identified previously in the evidence section is an example of a process measure.

Outcome measures are used to determine if the change idea achieved the desired results. Outcome measures can be identified as leading or lagging. Leading indicators are near-term summative assessments. For example, a test at the end of a unit of instruction would be a leading measure. Lagging indicators are long-term summative assessments. End-of-year state testing is an example of a lagging indicator. For the data collection section of the template, the teacher(s) must identify the name of the data collection tool and what data the tool will collect.

With these sections of the template completed, near the beginning of the evaluation cycle the teacher leader should seek approval from the appropriate administrator. If revisions are required, they are made and the plan is resubmitted. If no revisions are required, then the teacher leader proceeds to implementing the action steps and begins collecting data.

**Results and Recommendations.** After completing the action steps and collecting data, the next step is examination of the results. The template contains five prompts. Each prompt is intended to facilitate a different aspect of thinking regarding the change outcomes. The first prompt relates to the fidelity of implementation. More specifically, did you (or the team) carry out the plan as proposed? Changes made along the way may have had a significant impact on results. Thus, changes made must be identified and recorded.

Prompt 2 requires reflection on any surprising or confusing results. If there are no surprising or confusing results, then this section can be left blank. Prompt 3 requires a summary of the results as well as determination of the match between those results and the original predictions. The focus for reflection of the fourth prompt is on recommendations: What, if anything, should be done differently based on the results of the actions in this plan? Lastly, the fifth prompt focuses on what the teacher leader learned from the implementation of this plan.

| Teacher Leader Name: | |
|---|---|
| Supervisor Name: | Plan Start/End Dates: |
| Team Project (if applicable, list members—if not, put N/A) | |

**IDENTIFIED AREA FOR PROGRAM GROWTH**

S.M.A.R.T Goal: What am I (or we) trying to accomplish? For whom? By how much? By when?

Change Idea(s): What change(s) can I (or we) make that will result in improvement?

Evidence: I (We) will know that this change idea is an improvement because teachers and/or students will…..

Prediction: I (We) predict that teachers and/or students will….

**ACTION PLAN**

| ACTION STEPS | WHOM | WHEN |
|---|---|---|
| | | |
| | | |
| | | |
| | | |
| | | |
| | | |

**DATA COLLECTION PLAN**

| Data Collection Tool | Data to be Collected |
|---|---|
| | |
| | |
| | |

**INITIAL APPROVAL**

| Date of Initial Approval: |
|---|
| Teacher Leader's Signature: |
| Supervisor's Signature: |

Figure 2.1    Teacher-Leader Program Growth Objective Form.

| RESULTS |
| --- |
| Were the action steps completed as planned? If not, what was different? |
| What did you conclude or observe that surprised or confused you? |
| What were the results? How did they match your prediction? |
| Do you have any recommendations based on the results? If so, what are they and why? |
| What did you learn from conducting this plan? |
| **FINAL REVIEW** |
| Date of Final Review: |
| Teacher Leader's Signature: |
| Supervisor's Signature: |

Figure 2.1 (Continued)

**Teacher-Leader Portfolio.** Portfolios provide teacher leaders with opportunities for self-reflection. In addition, they can be helpful tools for assessing the quality of services provided. However, to achieve these aims they must be more than a miscellaneous collection of artifacts or an extended list of professional activities. Portfolios must carefully and thoughtfully document a set of accomplishments attained over an extended period of time.

In addition, it is important to carefully select the contents of the finished portfolio so that it is manageable for both the person who constructs it and the person who reviews it. The requirements of this portfolio are designed to encourage reflection while minimizing the quantity of material included.

**Teacher-Leader Portfolio Directions:**

1. The teacher leader is required to submit a portfolio containing the following elements:
   a. Reflective writing focused on the corresponding goals of the year.
   b. Required Elements:
      i. Client Survey Summary Form 1 and 2.
      ii. Program Growth Objective Form.
      iii. Three choice items selected by the teacher.
2. This portfolio must be submitted to the teacher leader's evaluator at least ten days prior to the summative evaluation conference.
3. The goal of this portfolio is to be concise and reflective. The teacher leader may not add additional elements or go beyond the stated requirements.
4. The teacher leader should receive feedback on the quality of this portfolio during their summative evaluation conference.

## TEACHER LEADERSHIP PORTFOLIO

This portfolio is a collection of your work. It represents you and the work that you have done during this school year. Some of the work will need to be selected, while other work will need to be created for this portfolio. For work which you select, staple on top a cover sheet that explains to the reader *what the selection is, what you thought of it, what you learned from it,* and anything else you would like to include. Each cover sheet must be between one and three paragraphs.

1. **Cover Letter**: Give the reader an introduction to you and your portfolio. Include *one separate paragraph* for each of the following:
   a. Describe how you have grown and improved as a teacher leader over the course of the school year.
   b. Describe an area of responsibility that you need to continue working on or improving at. Include a description of how you intend to achieve this goal.
   c. Describe an achievement you accomplished this year that you are proud of. What was the achievement, how did you accomplish it, and why you are proud of it?

2. **Required Elements:**
   a. Teacher Survey Summary Forms 1 and 2.
   b. Program Growth Objective Form.
3. **Choices**: (Be sure to include a cover sheet for each choice.)
   a. Choose an artifact that demonstrates how you improved student achievement.
   b. Choose an artifact that demonstrates how you improved the practice of peers.
   c. Choose an artifact that demonstrates how you have improved collaboration and relational trust with those you work with.
4. **Presentation:**
   a. Include a table of contents and make sure your work is submitted in order.

(Staple to inside front cover of manila folder.)
**Total Score:** _____ /9

Table 2.2  Teacher Leader Portfolio Scoring Rubric

| | Portfolio Assessment Form | | | |
| --- | --- | --- | --- | --- |
| | Score 3.0 | Score 2.0 | Score 1.0 | Score 0 |
| Cover Letter | Three separate paragraphs, each of which meets *all* of the specified requirements. | Three separate paragraphs, each of which meets *most* of the specified requirements. | Three separate paragraphs, each of which meets *some* of the specified requirements. | No cover letter included or missing entire required sections. |
| Required Elements | All of the elements required are submitted. The reflection for each item is thoughtful and comprehensive. | All of the elements required are submitted; however, at least some aspects of the reflections are superficial. | Some of the required elements are submitted. | None of the required elements are submitted. |
| Choices | Three items selected, each of which has a cover sheet that meets *all* of the specified requirements. | Three items selected, each of which has a cover sheet that meets *most* of the specified requirements. | Three items selected, each of which has a cover sheet that meets *some* of the specified requirements. | Missing one or more of the required choices. |

(Staple to inside rear cover of manila folder.)

## Teacher-Leader Summative Rating Forms

1. Each domain contains a rubric-based rating scale that is to be used to evaluate teacher-leader performance over time (figure 2.2).
2. Observational data and teacher reflection products are combined to make a summative judgment of the teacher leader's performance. This

**SUMMATIVE EVALUATION – TEACHER LEADER**

| Name of Staff Member: | School year: |
|---|---|
| Name of Evaluator: | Date of Summative Conference: |

| Domain 1: Interpersonal and Communication Skills | | | |
|---|---|---|---|
| Highly Effective | Effective | Partially Effective | Ineffective |
| Use of exemplary interpersonal and communication strategies results in strong interpersonal relationships; clear, concise, and timely communication; and highly productive group work. | Consistently uses effective interpersonal and communication strategies to build relationships, communicate information, and help groups accomplish tasks. | Attempts to use interpersonal and communication strategies, but results are partially effective and/or use of strategies is inconsistent. | Does not use interpersonal and communication strategies to build relationships, communicate information, and help groups accomplish tasks. |
| Comments: | | | |

| Domain 2: Professional Learning and Growth | | | |
|---|---|---|---|
| Highly Effective | Effective | Partially Effective | Ineffective |
| Use of extensive knowledge of the characteristics of adult learners and change management strategies results in systemic professional learning that can be linked to significant student achievement gains. | Consistently uses knowledge of the characteristics of adult learners and change management strategies to promote the professional learning of colleagues. | Attempts to use knowledge of characteristics of adult learners and change management strategies but results are partially effective and/or use of strategies is inconsistent. | Does not use knowledge of the characteristics of adult learners and/or change management strategies to promote the professional learning of colleagues. |
| Comments: | | | |

Figure 2.2 Summative Evaluation—Teacher Leader.

summative judgment can lead to additional professional development opportunities and/or decisions regarding renewal of employment.
3. Domains 1, 5, 6, and 7 will be evaluated for all teacher leaders. Of the remaining domains, only those relevant to the teacher leader's job responsibilities should receive a score.

| Domain 3: Instructional Leadership | | | |
|---|---|---|---|
| Highly Effective | Effective | Partially Effective | Ineffective |
| Use of exemplary data analysis strategies, coaching skills, and curriculum knowledge promotes demonstrable and significant gains in student achievement. | Consistently uses data, coaching skills, and knowledge of curriculum to promote continuous improvement of instruction. | Attempts to use data, coaching skills, and/or knowledge of curriculum, but results are partially effective and/or use of strategies is inconsistent. | Does not use data, coaching skills, and/or knowledge of curriculum to promote continuous improvement of instruction. |
| Comments: | | | |

| Domain 4: Human Resources Management | | | |
|---|---|---|---|
| Highly Effective | Effective | Partially Effective | Ineffective |
| Use of organizational skills, professional judgment, and communication skills results in significant measurable improvement of the school recruitment, selection, orientation, and mentoring process. | Consistently uses organizational skills, professional judgment, and communication skills to assist with the recruitment, selection, orientation, and mentoring of new staff members. | Attempts to use organizational skills, professional judgment and communication skills, but results are partially effective and/or use of strategies is inconsistent. | Does not use organizational skills, professional judgment and/or communication skills to assist with the recruitment, selection, orientation, and mentoring of new staff members. |
| Comments: | | | |

Figure 2.2  (Continued)

| Domain 5: School Community and Advocacy ||||
| --- | --- | --- | --- |
| Highly Effective | Effective | Partially Effective | Ineffective |
| Uses sophisticated understanding of school culture and politics to significantly influence school climate and achieve desired outcomes. | Consistently and ethically uses knowledge of school culture and politics to positively influence school climate and achieve desired outcomes. | Attempts to use knowledge of school culture and politics, but results are partially effective or attempts are haphazard. | Does not use knowledge of school culture and politics to positively influence school climate and achieve desired outcomes, or acts in a manner that is unethical. |
| Comments: ||||

| Domain 6: Professionalism ||||
| --- | --- | --- | --- |
| Highly Effective | Effective | Partially Effective | Ineffective |
| Demonstrates grace under pressure. Applies knowledge and skills from professional learning activities to make significant and measurable student or program gains. Contributes in a significant and meaningful way to the profession. | Consistently and effectively maintains a professional demeanor, participates in professional learning activities, and makes contributions to the profession. | Attempts to maintain a professional demeanor, participate in professional learning activities, and contribute to the profession, but results are inconsistent. | Demonstrates unprofessional behavior. |
| Comments: ||||

**Figure 2.2** (Continued)

| Domain 7: Student/Program Progress ||||
| Highly Effective | Effective | Partially Effective | Ineffective |
|---|---|---|---|
| The work of the teacher leader results in student and/or program progress that significantly exceeds expectations on challenging goals. | The work of the teacher leader results in acceptable, measurable student and/or program progress based on established personal, school, and/or district goals. | The work of the teacher leader results in meaningful progress towards personal, school, and/or district goals, but one or more goals were not achieved. | The work of the teacher leader results in insufficient student and/or program progress. |
| Comments: ||||
| Staff Member's Comments (If more space is needed, please attach documents to this form.) ||||
| Supervisor's Signature: || Date: ||
| Staff Member's Signature: || Date: ||

**Figure 2.2 (Continued)**

The content of this chapter has provided the reader with both recommendations and rationale for creating conditions that support teacher leadership. More specifically, in order for teacher leadership to thrive, there must be a supportive school culture and administration. In addition, teacher leaders must be provided with both adequate time and professional development so that they may complete their responsibilities. Finally, teacher leaders must receive incentives and recognition as well as an evaluation process that serves to motivate and guide performance. Starting with interpersonal and communication skills, subsequent chapters will focus on the specific skills teacher leaders need to successfully perform their responsibilities.

*Chapter 3*

# Collaborative and Interpersonal Skill Development

Teacher leaders do not have formal authority. They cannot direct someone to do something because of the power of their position. Instead, teacher leaders must develop trusting and collaborative relationships in order to influence colleagues. The primary tools teacher leaders rely on to build these relationships are interpersonal and communication skills. Regardless of the assigned task responsibilities, teacher leaders will only be successful if they develop proficiency with these skills. Interpersonal and communication skills are the foundation of successful teacher leadership.

In the previous chapter, the relationship between school administration and teacher leadership was addressed. This chapter will focus on building relationships with colleagues. More specifically, the first part of this chapter will describe the skills required for effective, individual, interpersonal communication. The second part of the chapter will describe the skills required for leading groups.

As noted in chapter 2, cultural norms can make it difficult to form positive and productive relationships between teacher leaders and other faculty members. Yet, colleagues must be willing to work alongside teacher leaders if these leaders are to have a significant impact on the school-wide instructional program. Teacher leaders can cope more effectively with faculty resistance if they realize it is usually not personal and requires both time and patience to overcome.

Teachers are their own worst enemy when it comes to unlocking leadership opportunities because they often don't welcome or respect it and often feel threatened by one of their own taking it (Barth, 2013). If the teacher leader was promoted from within, some colleagues may resent them for advancing their careers. Those that were the teacher leader's friends at some point may now see them as a "traitor" or "sellout."

If the teacher leader was brought in from outside the school, they will surely face resistance. Among other things, this resistance can take the form of opposing new ideas, dampening enthusiasm, blocking discussions, and discouraging problem-solving. Because other teachers do not want one of their own to lead or stand out, they engage in active or passive efforts to "pull down" teacher leaders.

Despite the desire to comprehend the situation, teacher leaders must acknowledge that they may never understand the motives for the treatment they receive from some faculty members. Leadership breeds envy, and that envy would likely be targeted at anyone assuming a teacher-leader role.

If the behavior of colleagues rises to the level of open hostility or subversive actions that make it impossible for the teacher leader to complete assigned tasks, then it is appropriate to involve a direct supervisor. If the behavior is petty, then the best approach for teacher leaders to take when dealing with detractors is to ignore it. Demonstrating unwillingness to be deterred by negative colleagues both annoys the detractors and earns the respect of colleagues that feel either neutral or positive about teacher leadership. You may even eventually win over some of the faculty members that initially resisted your efforts.

**Communication Skills.** In order to be an effective communicator, a teacher leader must become fluent in the use of six core interpersonal skills. Effective teacher leaders demonstrate the ability to listen, ask questions, make statements, give and receive feedback, and use nonverbal communications. Providing feedback is an important communication skill that will be addressed as part of the discussion on instructional coaching in chapter 6. Throughout this section, each of the other five skills will be addressed separately. The information is structured in this manner to improve the quality of the explanations. In reality, these skills are used simultaneously as part of attempts to communicate effectively.

**Active Listening.** As I observe the communication that occurs between many teachers, I am reminded of the concept of parallel play. However, instead of children playing, it is adults simultaneously or alternately talking without much, if any, regard for the other party. The speakers take turns talking and acting as an audience for each other without responding in any meaningful way to what the other person communicates. Obviously, this pattern of communication does not lead to the development of collaborative relationships.

Effectively building rapport and relationships with colleagues requires the use of active listening strategies. Active listening is a process during which the listener sends back to the message-sender signals indicating what the listener thinks the sender meant (Harris, 2002). In active listening, the receiver of the message becomes part of the transaction and assumes active responsibility for understanding the thoughts and feelings of the message sender.

Unlike "parallel" conversations, active listening does establish rapport and helps build relationships (Seeley, 2005). Active listening has this effect because it is a demonstration of concern for the speaker as an individual as well as an indication of the desire to understand the other person's perception of the situation. On the other hand, a hasty or inaccurate response to a speaker's comments implies little concern for their perception of the issue and even less concern for the person as an individual.

A second benefit of active listening is that it also makes it possible to obtain the sufficient level of accurate information necessary for engaging in a collaborative dialogue. Without this sufficient level of accurate information, it is difficult, if not impossible, to reach a solution that meets the needs of both parties.

The following three factors are obstacles that may interfere with the ability to employ active listening skills. First, we are all capable of receiving information through listening at a faster rate than the average speaker can convey (Friend & Cook, 2007). As a result, the listener has additional time to think while they are trying to listen. This additional thinking time, which may be used for daydreaming about any number of activities, may lead to losing track of the speaker's message.

Second, as the speaker is talking it is tempting for the listener to mentally engage in framing their response. In other words, having caught the drift of the message being sent, the listener mentally proceeds to prepare what they will say once it is their turn to speak. As a result of this mental diversion, the listener misses aspects of what the speaker is saying.

Third, it may be difficult to listen because attention is being drawn away from the message being conveyed. For example, suppose the individual speaking has a strong accent. As the listener, it may be more difficult to focus on the words being spoken because of the distraction caused by the nature of the accent. Any physical, verbal, or environmental distraction will interfere with the ability to actively listen (Friend & Cook, 2007).

Considering these barriers, the first step toward improving active listening skills is to mentally prepare for listening. Prior to speaking with a colleague about an important issue, an attempt must be made by the teacher leader to deliberately shut out competing thoughts. Mentally, the listener must prepare to direct their attention to the speaker. While this is a necessary first step, it is difficult to do in emotionally charged situations.

As a colleague is speaking, there are three types of statements a teacher leader can make that will demonstrate they are listening. The first type of statement a teacher leader can make is paraphrasing. When paraphrasing, the listener restates in their own words what they believe the sender has said. The focus of the paraphrase is on relatively small units of information and there are little or no inferences made. Paraphrasing does not imply agreement with the sender's message, only an attempt to demonstrate accurate understanding of the content of the message. Consider the following example in which a teacher leader paraphrases a concern expressed by a teacher.

**Teacher:** Your idea for using cooperative learning structures will never work with my students. They are too immature to work together.
**Teacher Leader:** You believe that your students are too immature to do cooperative learning activities. (Inflection indicates the tentative nature of this response and suggests a querying attitude.)

A second, more complex statement the listener can make to demonstrate they are listening involves the use of reflection. When reflecting, not only does the listener restate what the speaker has said, he or she also uses additional words in an attempt to capture the affective message. Imagine that the previous conversation between the teacher and the teacher leader has continued:

**Teacher:** Yes, not only are they too immature, it will take too much time to do and I am already behind according to the curriculum pacing guide.
**Teacher Leader:** You believe that using cooperative learning activities will lead you to fall further behind the curriculum guide expectations. I sense that you are anxious about this.

Through restating the teacher's message and reflecting their feelings, the teacher leader has conveyed understanding of the situation from the teacher's point of view. Not only has he or she conveyed an accurate understanding of the teacher's viewpoint, but they have also demonstrated an understanding of, and value for, the teacher's feelings.

The final type of statement the listener can make to demonstrate they are actively listening involves summarizing. When summarizing, the listener concisely restates several of the key points made during the interaction. Unlike paraphrasing and reflecting, summarizing is a response to several pieces of information, often presented by more than one speaker. Picture the teacher leader from the above-mentioned exchange as he or she summarizes the concerns expressed by a group of colleagues.

**Teacher Leader:** Let's see if we agree on the main points shared so far. Jane, you are concerned that your students are too immature to use cooperative learning structures and that you will fall farther behind the curriculum pacing guide if you use them. Sandy, you believe that it is not the responsibility of the teacher to instruct students in social skills, that is something that should be done by their parents. Is this an accurate understanding of the main points shared thus far?

The final question in the aforementioned example demonstrates the use of checking for accuracy. When checking for accuracy, the listener asks for confirmation that the summary statement made is correct. It is one way to enhance the probability that those involved in the interaction have a shared perception of what has been stated. Whenever the listener is in doubt about the content of their paraphrasing, reflecting, or summarizing statements, they should check for accuracy.

**Questioning.** The ability to effectively ask the right questions can make the difference between a successful, collaborative interaction and one that is fraught with misunderstandings and miscommunication. In order to create the right question, teacher leaders should consider two dimensions. The first dimension to consider is a decision on whether the question should be open- or closed-ended.

Open-ended questions are designed to get the individual being communicated with to share the general information sought. These types of questions should be used to elicit an elaborate response. Examples of open-ended questions include:

- How do you think the expectations you have for your students influence their ability to use cooperative learning structures?
- What would understanding of this mathematical concept look like?
- Why do you think the team hasn't started to plan interdisciplinary units of instruction?

Used early in a conversation, well-structured, open-ended questions will elicit volumes of information. By having teachers elaborate on a topic, you are gaining valuable insights required for understanding. The drawback to using open-ended questions is that they enable the speaker to go off on tangents, which are sometimes unrelated to the topic of discussion.

Closed-ended questions are designed to obtain very specific information and answers. These types of questions should be used to limit the scope of information shared or to confirm the accuracy of information. Examples of closed-ended questions include:

- Did you use the think-pair-share strategy in your lesson?
- Does your co-teacher get a copy of your lesson plan in advance?
- When are students given a copy of the assessment rubric?

Used after having developed a general understanding of the teacher's message, closed-ended questions prompt specific answers to issues not covered in the general conversation. Furthermore, closed-ended questions make it possible to steer the conversation in a specific direction.

The second dimension to consider when forming a question is whether the question should be direct or indirect. Most questions are asked using a direct format. If written, direct questions would end with a question mark. An example of a direct question is, "Heather, what do you think about that as a possibility?"

Because they are phrased as a statement, indirect questions do not query specific individuals. In addition, because they begin with the word "I," the person answering the question does not need to assume ownership for the idea expressed. An example of an indirect question is, "I wonder what would happen if we showed students examples of finished products at the beginning of our directions." Indirect questions are particularly appropriate when you are unsure if answering a direct question would be considered offensive, awkward, or uncomfortable.

A critical skill required for effectively asking questions is the use of pauses. Two particular uses of pauses can improve the effectiveness of question asking (Friend & Cook, 2007). The first is the use of a brief pause before asking a question. This pause enables the speaker to phrase the question so that it will convey the intended message. The second use is to pause after asking a question. This pause allows the person being questioned to think about, phrase, and then deliver his or her response. Even though it may feel awkward at first, the use of pauses can be a very effective strategy for obtaining information from a respondent.

**Making Statements.** Statements serve as the primary verbal method for providing information to others. Much like questions, the form and the substance of each statement will determine how it is perceived and understood by the listener. In order to meet the goal of effectively providing information, statements should be delivered with two characteristics.

The first characteristic of effective statements is that they are delivered in a manner that is as neutral as possible. More specifically, statements are delivered in a way that is neither judgmental nor evaluative. Contrast the following two statements:

**Statement A:** As a teacher, you need to provide a study guide for every exam. Lack of providing study guides is unacceptable and you are causing students to get poor grades.

**Statement B:** Your students are not scoring well on tests. Providing a study guide prior to the test could help the students be more prepared.

The information provided in Statement B is more likely to be received favorably by the listener. Unlike Statement A, this statement remains focused on the facts of the situation. By avoiding judgment of the actions of those involved, the speaker of Statement B can avoid provoking the distractions associated with defensive behaviors.

Imprecise language is often the cause of miscommunication. A language that is vague may obscure the information sent to the point that the listener cannot accurately determine the intent of the communication. Thus, the second characteristic of statements that promote understanding is their level of specificity. Statements focused on specific behaviors are more easily understood than general comments. For example, compare the following two statements:

**Statement A:** I was concerned about how you reacted last time.

**Statement B:** The last time we met, I presented you with data on your use of wait-time after asking questions. After I finished presenting the data, you expressed your disagreement with my data collection by raising your voice and making accusations about my intentions.

Unlike Statement B, Statement A does not provide any indication for the reason behind the speaker's concern. Thus, the listener receiving Statement A is left to draw his or her own conclusions. The conclusions drawn may or may not be an accurate understanding of the speaker's intended message. In general, the more concrete and precise the language used, the more likely it is the listener will understand the intended message.

Two types of statements that should generally be avoided when attempting to communicate with teachers are commands and unsolicited advice. Commands such as "you must write your learning objectives using this format" are usually negatively received. One reason for this negative reception is that a command implies the speaker has power over the listener. Even if this is true, commands are frequently met with either overt or covert resistance (Friend & Cook, 2007).

Similarly, providing advice to someone who has not requested it is unlikely to be helpful. Statements of advice like "you really should spend more time reading professional literature" are frequently perceived as arrogant and intrusive. Furthermore, unsolicited advice tends to make those receiving it feel misunderstood and defensive.

**Giving and Receiving Feedback.** At some point, teacher leaders will receive feedback about the quality or nature of their work. Regardless of whether this feedback is solicited or not, it is important for the teacher leader to receive the feedback openly with a non-defensive posture. Demonstrating willingness to listen to feedback is important for establishing the perception of confidence and professionalism.

The first rule of receiving feedback is that the receiver does not have to agree with the content of the message sent. Instead, the role of the feedback receiver is to strive to understand the message the speaker is sending. The receiver should remain open to the fact that someone else might be interpreting things differently than they are. In addition, it is frequently worthwhile to take time to reflect on the feedback received. While it is certainly appropriate to ask for clarification when any aspect of the message is unclear, it is not necessary to respond at that moment. Taking time to process the feedback allows the receiver of the message to take some of the emotion out of the interaction.

Upon reflection, if the feedback receiver believes aspects of the viewpoint provided are valid, then it is appropriate to acknowledge this agreement. Willingness to admit mistakes or acknowledge shortcomings can go a long way toward building relational trust.

**Nonverbal Behaviors.** Nonverbal behaviors are powerful communication mechanisms. One specific nonverbal behavior that can be especially powerful for promoting collaboration is a technique called mirroring. Mirroring is the ability to match the other person's verbal and nonverbal behavior.

The first step of mirroring is to accurately assess the other person's verbal and nonverbal behaviors. Specific verbal behaviors to identify include the tempo, rate, and volume of their speech. Specific nonverbal behaviors to identify include body posture and gestures.

Once identified, the listener will then match those behaviors. In other words, if the speaker is quick and to the point, then the listener will also be quick and to the point. If the speaker leans back in his chair and appears relaxed, the listener will attempt to do the same. It is critically important for the listener to use subtlety when mirroring. If the listener is not subtle then the speaker may perceive that they are being mocked, and thus may become offended.

To determine if the listener and speaker have established rapport, the listener should adjust their behavior and notice if the speaker does the same. If the speaker follows the listener's lead, they probably have established rapport. If the speaker does not mirror the listener's lead, then the listener will need to do additional mirroring of the speaker's behavior. Regardless of how it is achieved, once you have established this rapport you have triggered a strong, automatic positive reaction within your communication partner (Granger, 2008).

**Leading Groups.** Teacher leaders will be part of more diverse types of groups than they were in their role as purely classroom teachers. In their new role, teacher leaders may be members of various types of school and district governance teams. In addition, they may be thrust into the role of leader for grade levels, departments, and committees. Effective group leadership is critical for gaining the benefits of faculty collaboration. Therefore, teacher leaders must develop the knowledge and skills associated with leading groups.

Effective group leadership begins with understanding the dynamics of group development. Groups develop over time, hopefully progressing through stages of development. The speed at which teams progress through these stages will vary depending on their size, complexity of their tasks, the personalities of the members, and the circumstances of the situation. Furthermore, while these stages are common in new groups, they also may reoccur when mature groups encounter new problems, issues, or tasks.

The following five stages are not purely linear, as aspects of one stage continue to appear as the next stage emerges (Carr et al., 2005). Furthermore, not all groups get to the final stages as they may get bogged down in the conflict associated with early stages (Levi, 2007). Teacher leaders cannot force group members to become high-performing teams, but they can provide the context and structure necessary for promoting high productivity.

**Stages of Group Development.** The first stage of group development is called the forming stage. Forming is the process of coming together as a group, getting acquainted, settling into the group's identity, and having each member embrace his or her own role in, and importance to, the group. In this stage, group members are generally guarded and cordial to one another. Storming is the second stage of group development. This is the stage in which differences in styles and goals emerge. Group members may bid for control and rebel against the leadership of the teacher leader as well as their fellow group members. They may form cliques or factions and take sides. At this point, neither side listens to nor appreciates the viewpoint of the other.

The third stage, norming, is the one in which group members work out expectations for how they will operate. When they have reached this stage, group members generally accept the rules and standards for group behavior. However, group members may still not demonstrate open support for one another.

Performing is the stage in which the group gets the majority of its work done. At this point, the group moves forward with its work, acting cooperatively instead of competitively. The final stage of group development is adjourning. This is the point at which the task is completed and the group disbands.

Four ideas related to these stages are important for team leaders if they are to help a group reach the performing stage. First, emotional highs and lows are a normal part of group development. The team leader cannot overreact to these highs or lows but instead must maintain an appropriate emotional perspective.

Second, purposeful development of the group is vital. Early in the group's life cycle, time must be devoted to social relations and socializing new members. These actions are especially critical in the forming stage of group development. Ice-breakers and warm-up activities can be effective tools for helping group members become more open and relaxed with one another.

Third, the teacher leader must facilitate goal setting and the development of operational norms prior to attempting to focus on task completion. Having agreed-upon goals and operating norms becomes important when the conflict associated with the storming phase emerges. The problem is not the presence of conflict; rather, it is getting stuck in it. Clear goals and agreed-upon operating norms kept at the forefront of discussions can help address unproductive conflicts.

Lastly, the group is likely to go through periods of low task performance. At times, the focus of group members' energy will be on conflicts over relationships and task issues. This is a normal part of group development and thus cannot be ignored or avoided. Instead, the team leader must employ appropriate conflict-management strategies to facilitate resolution of disagreements.

**Meeting Leadership Skills.** Groups tend to exercise their responsibilities through meetings. Unfortunately, few things in education are more common than poorly run meetings. Not only do poorly run meetings produce poor outcomes, but they are demoralizing. Efficient and effective meetings can have quite the opposite effect. This section focuses on the knowledge and technical skills required to lead quality group meetings, beginning with two tasks that must be completed early in the group's life cycle.

**Team Purpose.** Possessing a clear understanding of the group's purpose as expressed through well-articulated goals is a common characteristic of successful teams (Levi, 2007). Clarity of expected outcomes enables group members to align their efforts to achieve tasks. In addition, with less confusion regarding performance expectations, one potential source of conflict is avoided. In advance of the group's first meeting, teacher leaders must work with group sponsors to clearly identify expected outcomes.

A common mistake is for groups to immediately begin their work without clarity of the task expectations. In their rush toward task completion, groups often spend too little time understanding the expected outcomes. Thus, groups often have to back up to earlier stages when confusion arises. Teacher leaders must ensure that every group member has the same understanding of the expected outcomes prior to starting work on the task.

**Ground Rules.** The second task to be completed early in the group's life cycle is establishing ground rules for group behavior. Ground rules are the agreed-upon norms by which group members agree to operate. Identifying and agreeing upon ground rules at the outset establishes an efficient approach to getting the job done and creates a safe working environment in which differences of opinion can be resolved. In addition, groups benefit from discussing and establishing norms at the beginning of their work because it prevents the development of inappropriate behaviors and makes everyone aware of the type of behavior expected.

Teacher leaders can facilitate the adoption of ground rules in at least two ways. First, they can lead the group in brainstorming potential ground rules. Second, the teacher leader can provide a draft list of potential ground rules for discussion. In either case, the teacher leader must work with group members to revise and adapt the rules so that they best suit the needs of the group. The clearer and more specific the norm, the more likely it is that members will conform to it (Levi, 2007).

After the ground rules are agreed upon, they should be enforced fairly and consistently. Violations of agreed-upon rules should be addressed tactfully and, if possible, privately. Sometimes a simple reminder of the rule being violated is enough to change behavior. Other times, a one-on-one meeting is necessary to address the reasons for and consequences of the behavior. If a facilitator is to maintain credibility as a group leader, they must demonstrate the ability to appropriately address violations of agreed-upon group ground rules.

**Meeting Roles.** Recurring meeting responsibilities can be assigned as roles. Roles can increase meeting efficiency and ensure that specific tasks are accomplished. Three common roles for meetings are facilitator, recorder, and timekeeper.

The facilitator is usually (but not always) the teacher leader. He or she is responsible for formalizing the meeting agenda, starting and ending the meeting on time, and introducing each agenda item in turn. In addition to naming the agenda item, the facilitator describes the method to be used and the amount of time allotted for that item. He or she uses facilitation skills to ensure that information is shared, understood, and processed by the team in a supportive and participative environment.

The facilitator is responsible for structuring the team's interactions, but is not responsible for doing all the talking or making all the decisions at a meeting. On the other hand, as a member of a group, the teacher leader has the right to express his or her opinions and preferences.

When advocating for a position, the teacher leader's goal is to make their thinking and reasoning visible to others as they strive to test assumptions and conclusions. This is done by stating an assumption, describing the reasoning that led to that assumption, and encouraging others to examine the thought process. For example, "I think that we should select option A. I come to this conclusion because it is the most cost-effective and it will reach the most students. Do you see it differently?"

The recorder creates minutes of the meeting, including key decisions, next steps, and task assignments. The intention is not to capture the entire discussion. Instead, the minutes should serve as a record of the most important points and decisions. Minutes should be distributed to meeting participants within forty-eight hours of the meeting so that they may have the opportunity to seek clarification or request revisions if necessary. A timekeeper remains aware of the clock and warns fellow group members when the designated time for each agenda item is almost over. When a topic is not completed within the established time frame, the group should stop and formally decide whether to devote additional time or whether to add the item to a future agenda for further consideration.

These roles may be permanent or they can be rotated. Permanent role assignments have the advantage of consistency and of helping group members develop role-specific skills over time. Rotating assignments have the advantage of promoting equal responsibility among all staff members for all roles.

**Meeting Agenda.** A quality meeting begins with advanced preparation. This preparation commonly takes the form of developing a meeting agenda (see figure 3.1). An agenda is a written plan for how the meeting will happen and what the meeting is expected to accomplish. Every meeting should have an explicit agenda that communicates the following items:

- Meeting participants.
- Date, time, and location of the meeting.
- A short statement describing the purpose for the meeting.
- The names of those with identified meeting responsibilities (timekeeper, recorder, etc.).
- Name of agenda items listed in the order of importance.
- The name of the person leading the activity related to each item.
- Type of item or method to be used for that item.
- Description of expected outcomes relative to each item.

| Date of meeting: 12/13/2022 | Time of meeting: 9:30 – 10:00 |
|---|---|
| Location of meeting: Room 4 | Participants: Team Leaders & Dr. Smith |
| Recorder: Jane | Timekeeper: Vicki |
| Purpose of meeting: Review of options for providing Tier 2 assistance to struggling learners. | |

| Time | Item | Who | Method | Description/Outcome |
|---|---|---|---|---|
| 8:00 – 8:10 | Reading Interventions | Heidi | Report | Share sub team's conclusions from research. |
| 8:10 – 8:20 | DIBELS | Dr. Smith | Report | Update on implementation of DIBELS for progress monitoring. |
| 8:20 – 8:30 | Next Steps | Tim | Discussion | Discuss what was learned and make decisions about next steps. |

Figure 3.1   Sample Meeting Agenda.

As a general rule, general information should be disseminated through email or as an addendum to the agenda that people can read on their own. Meetings should be held for a purpose that cannot be accomplished through written communication. In addition, the agenda should be distributed to participants at least twenty-four hours in advance of the meeting. This action makes it possible for meeting participants to come to the meeting fully prepared to participate.

**Meeting Facilitation.** If a group needs to achieve a goal in a short period of time, or if a situation is particularly difficult, a direct style of meeting leadership may be necessary. In this case, the teacher leader serving as the group facilitator may need to control the discussion, making sure that decisions are made in a timely manner. However, this situation is typically the exception, not the rule. More commonly, meetings will involve a process of discussion focused on developing a common understanding.

Facilitating dialogue among group members is a critical teacher leader skill. In addition to the interpersonal skills described in the first section of the chapter, there are several additional techniques a teacher leader can employ to foster dialogue. Basic techniques designed to facilitate discussion include the following:

- Clarifying. If you are unclear about what someone has said or think that staff members may be unclear, ask the speaker to explain what he or she means. (Example: We would like to understand your view on the issue. Can you explain it differently so that we can gain a better understanding?)
- Leading. This technique is effective for introducing new topics or moving discussions forward. (Example: Now that we have brainstormed possible solutions to this problem, are we ready to make a decision?)
- Challenging. Use this technique to question underlying assumptions or unstated biases that are keeping the group from moving forward. (Example: Are we sure that we cannot hire substitute teachers to rotate among staff so that we can create common planning time?)
- Stretching: This is an effective technique for pushing a group to think differently about a situation. (Example: Have we considered other possible ways to assess student progress in math?)
- Connecting. Use this technique to share information or strategies that the group isn't actively considering. (Example: Samantha, last year your team created an interdisciplinary unit of study that combined art, music, and math. Would you please share with the group the process your team used to create this project?)
- Integrating. This technique can be used to merge ideas and conversations into an integrated whole. (Example: The situation you are describing is similar to the one we discussed at the end of last week's meeting.)

Regardless of the methods used, there are two overarching guidelines to always be mindful of when facilitating discussion. First, keep the group on track. When the group drifts into tangents on irrelevant subjects, politely redirect the conversation. Second, avoid allowing individuals to dominate the discussion. In order to be inclusive, all members' views must receive a thorough and respectful hearing.

Expression of diverse views commonly results in differences of opinion. Differences of opinion ultimately lead to disagreement and, potentially, conflict. For this reason, teacher leaders must develop the ability to manage group conflict productively.

**Managing Conflict.** Conflict in groups is not only inevitable but also desirable. When people are critical of ideas, it causes the group to examine topics from different viewpoints, further strengthening understanding. Diversity of opinions must be viewed as a positive aspect of group work. After all, if everyone has the same opinion, then what is the point of having a group discussion?

It is how conflict is handled that determines if it is destructive or constructive to the group's goals. Destructive conflict occurs when group members make personal attacks. This type of conflict is detrimental to the group because it destroys relationships and takes the focus away from achieving group goals.

Destructive conflict usually emanates from personality differences, competition for power, miscommunication, or long-held resentments. Sometimes the attack is a result of situational factors, as is the case when someone is experiencing high levels of stress due to work or personal issues. Other times, the presence of destructive conflict is indicative of underlying issues. Therefore, a teacher leader cannot assume that the apparent issue is the only source of the conflict, and should consider exploring other issues that may be contributing to the conflict.

Regardless of the source, destructive conflict cannot be ignored, nor can it be tolerated. Ideas can be criticized; colleagues should not be. The teacher leader must strive to keep the content of disagreements focused on the issue being discussed.

Productive conflict focuses on the "what" of the problem and not the "who." When the conflict is about legitimate differences of opinion related to the team's task, then appropriate expression of these differences should be encouraged.

A teacher leader can manage conflict in group settings through de-escalation. More specifically, the teacher leader can listen actively, acknowledge people's feelings, and reframe the conflict so the focus remains on issues and not individuals.

In addition, they can encourage group members to stop seeing conflict solutions as either/or and begin seeing them both/and. If both parties' interests can be satisfied, the resulting integrative agreement will strengthen the durability of solutions and potentially strengthen group members' relationships. A final strategy a teacher leader can use to prevent conflict is the use of structured approaches for problem-solving and decision-making.

**Problem-Solving.** Some problems are simple and therefore require minimal time for generating potential solutions. When the stakes are low, time is critical, the issues are clear, and/or commitment to the decision is less important than getting on with the task, then processes such as presenting options and allowing for a majority vote is appropriate.

However, when resolution of the problem is important, the problem is complex, and/or staff buy-in to the ultimate decision is essential, then a consensus approach to deciding among alternatives is necessary. Consensus decision-making does not mean the selected option is the top choice of every group member. Rather, consensus results in a decision reached when most group members agree on a clear option and the few opposed believe they had a reasonable opportunity to influence the selection. Ultimately, through the consensus process, all group members must eventually agree to gift their support to the final decision.

Reaching consensus on how to solve a problem is a time-consuming, challenging task. It takes time for teacher leaders to learn these skills and even more time to become competent in their use. The first task the teacher leader must learn how to do is leading the group in developing an agreed-upon interpretation of the problem.

**Problem Statement.** A common mistake when attempting to solve problems is rushing to generate solutions without fully understanding the nature of the problem. Research on problem-solving reveals that the effectiveness of solutions increases by 85 percent once the true problem has been identified (Cloke & Goldsmith). For this reason, devoting adequate time to developing a clear, common, and accurate statement of the problem is the first step in the problem-solving process.

The teacher leader can facilitate this task by writing a draft statement of the problem in a location visible to all group members. The teacher leader then leads the group in dialogue about the problem statement. The problem statement is revised as necessary until group members agree that it is both accurate and clear. The final problem statement should be recorded and placed where it can easily be seen. This allows group members to refer to the statement throughout the rest of the problem-solving process.

**Problem Analysis.** The second step of the group problem-solving process involves the teacher leader facilitating identification of the sources of the problem. Using a series of "critical questions," the group interrogates the nature of the problem. Working through each question, the group records group members' thoughts so that they are visible to all. The following "critical questions" are examples that can be used to determine the cause of most school problems: Is the problem the result of

- interpersonal difficulties?
- how people are organized throughout the system?
- lack of competency?
- insufficient resources?
- the norms, values, habits, and traditions of the school culture?
- a lack of communication?

After interrogating the problem statement by working through each question, the teacher leader facilitates group members reaching conclusions based on the information shared. At this point, the group may decide it does not have enough information to generate potential solutions. If this is the case, the group must determine what information is needed and how it can be obtained. If the group decides that it has enough information to begin generating solutions, the original problem statement should still be reviewed to determine if any revisions are required.

**Generating Options.** If the group has developed a clear, accurate problem statement and agreed upon potential causes of the problem, then it is ready to move onto the idea-generation phase. Finding an effective solution depends on the group's ability to generate a sufficient number of high-quality alternatives. Because brainstorming is a group activity designed to stimulate creativity and surface diverse perspectives in a relatively short period of time, it meets this goal. However, in order for brainstorming to be effective, the group must adhere to the following guidelines:

- Aim for quantity—lots of ideas is better.
- No evaluation or criticism of ideas at this point.
- Piggyback on other ideas as appropriate.
- Do not repeat ideas.
- Do not attempt to sell or explain ideas.
- Keep going. Ideas that come later in the process may be the best ideas.

The brainstorming process begins with sharing a clear focus question. Often the sentence stem, "in what ways might we (fill in the problem)?" is effective for generating a useful list of potential solutions. Next, participants share ideas, with each idea recorded for all to see. The sharing of ideas can be done in several ways.

First, participants can share ideas verbally, as quickly as they occur to them. Second, ideas can be shared by group members in turn, with participants being allowed to pass if they do not have an idea to share. Third, participants can record ideas on self-stick notes (one per idea). This option provides the advantage of making it easier to sort and organize ideas into categories. If the option to use self-stick notes is used, then participants must write clearly, be concise, and make the writing large enough to be seen from several feet away.

Upon expiration of the allotted time, the group should engage in structured dialogue about the various options generated during brainstorming. The following list of questions, considered one at a time, can be used to lead this discussion: Which options

- require clarification?
- could be combined?
- exclude each other?

**Assessing Alternatives.** With a quantity of potential solutions identified, the group must narrow down and prioritize the items on the list. The following process can be used to accomplish this task. First, divide the number of items on the list by three and round up to the nearest whole number. For example, if there are thirty-eight potential items on the list, each group member will receive thirteen votes (39/3=13). Second, distribute the same number of colored sticky dots (all of the same color) as there are votes to each group member. Third, allow group members to place their dots next to the ideas they favor most. Group members can distribute their dots evenly or they can place more than one on an item. After all the dots are distributed, refine the list by eliminating items that received no or only a few votes.

If the refined list still has too many ideas for the group to reasonably consider, then the process can be repeated. This time the number of items on the reduced list is divided by three and the appropriate amount of a different colored dot is distributed. The process should continue until the list is narrowed down to between five and ten potential solutions.

Having narrowed down the list of potential solutions to a reasonable number, it is time to determine the criteria to be used for making a final decision. Criteria are judgments or rules used for evaluating options. Criteria are particularly helpful for determining whether an option is viable.

Sample criteria education groups can include the amount of time required, costs, numbers of staff required, ease of implementation, and potential effectiveness with students. The selected criteria are listed horizontally in the top columns of a decision matrix (see table 3.1). Each remaining option is listed vertically down the farthest left-hand column of the matrix.

Criteria are to be evaluated using the following scale:

- 5 = option fully meets the criteria
- 3 = option somewhat meets the criteria
- 1 = option does not meet the criteria

If some criteria are considered more important than others, then the group may decide to weigh those criteria. For example, if cost was most important, then the group could agree to multiply that score by two.

Working individually or as a group, move vertically through the table (by criteria) scoring all options against that criterion. Continue the process of scoring all options for each criterion until all of the columns are completed. Then total the score for each option by adding the scores for each criterion. Those with the highest scores best meet the stated criteria. In the following case, the option that best meets the stated criteria is the use of funds to add a chess club to the school's extracurricular activity program.

Table 3.1   Sample Decision Making Matrix

| Options | Cost | Ease of Implementation | Number of Students Impacted | Total Score |
|---|---|---|---|---|
| New Chess Club | 5 | 5 | 3 | 13 |
| New Fencing Team | 3 | 3 | 1 | 7 |
| Resurfacing the Track | 1 | 1 | 5 | 7 |

## Collaborative and Interpersonal Skill Development

**Choosing Solutions.** Having selected an option, it is time to inventory support for and identify concerns related to that option. An effective group listens to minority opinions. Often an aspect of the solution to a problem lies in the knowledge of a group member who is ignored because of the focus on the majority opinion (Levi, 2007). Using the "fist to five" method, each group member will have the opportunity to express their opinion. Explain to group members that they should raise the number of fingers based on the following scale:

- Five fingers indicate total agreement. This number of fingers should be displayed when the individual believes it is the best solution and they are willing to give it their complete support.
- Three fingers indicate the individual is willing to support the option. This number of fingers should be displayed when they could live with this option but they do have some concerns.
- A fist indicates the individual is unwilling to support the option. A fist is displayed when the individual has serious concerns and prefers that the group does not select this option.

After asking group members to display their level of support, the facilitator's next step will depend upon the majority response. If the majority of the hands showed all five fingers, then the following process should be used:

- Ask those with a fist to say why it is not possible to accept the option. Record the responses so they can be seen by all group members.
- Ask those with three fingers showing to express their concerns. Once again, record the responses.
- Ask some of those with five fingers showing to speak for the option.
- Engage the group in a discussion about the option to give team members that expressed a three-finger or fist opinion the opportunity to influence those who expressed five fingers of support.

If the majority of hands show three fingers or a fist:

- Ask the group members with five fingers to state why they support the decision. Record the responses.
- Ask some of those displaying three fingers to share their reasons. Record the responses.
- Ask some of those showing a fist to share their reasons. Record the responses.
- Conduct a team discussion to give the group members displaying five fingers of support the opportunity to influence those who displayed a

fist or three fingers. Attempt to problem-solve concerns raised by group members.

If there is no clear majority:

- Gather a sample or reasons for all three different levels of opinion. Record all comments.
- Facilitate a group discussion in which everyone has the opportunity to influence others. Attempt to address concerns and reasons for lack of support.
- If appropriate, have a second fist to five vote to determine if anything changed as a result of the discussion. If not, it will be necessary to continue the dialogue until a jointly invented solution that satisfies everyone's interests has been reached.

Once everyone has indicated at least three fingers of support, the group can declare they have reached consensus. At this point, if necessary, the group can move to creating an action plan for implementing the decision.

Even after the group reaches consensus, it can be useful to conduct a second-chance meeting a few days later. A second-chance meeting provides the opportunity to air concerns that arose after having time to reflect on the decision.

The content of this chapter has provided teacher leaders with the knowledge and skills needed for building relationships with colleagues, communicating information, and facilitating group accomplishment of tasks. The focus of the next chapter is developing the knowledge of the characteristics of adult learners and change management strategies in order to promote the professional learning of colleagues.

*Chapter 4*

# Mapping the Terrain
## *"School Politics and Culture"*

Make no mistake, all school systems are political. There are two interrelated reasons why this is so. First, because of their structure and function, schools are inevitably coalitions of different individuals and groups. Each coalition is characterized by enduring differences in their values, beliefs, and interests. Second, school resources are limited. Thus, choices must be made for how these limited resources will be allocated.

The interplay between coalitions with different interests and the limits on resources inevitably leads to conflict within the organizational system. In other words, every group wants certain things, but there is almost never enough to go around. The real question is not whether a school or district is political, but rather how ethically and effectively the politics are managed.

If teacher leaders are to acquire essential resources and promote the agenda they believe is best for their school, then they must develop political power. Just because teacher leaders have been given a position that bestows a certain amount of individual power, they should not believe that this will be enough to accomplish important goals. Instead, teacher leaders must diagnose the relative power of various organizational members, identify patterns of interdependence, and build their level of influence.

Teacher leaders must know how to build alliances and networks. These connections will help pull together the people, funding, and other resources needed to support action plans. Teacher leaders must know the social dynamics within their school and how to connect like-minded people as well as how to work with skeptics (Katzenmyer & Moller, 2009).

**Mapping the Terrain.** Prior to making any significant decisions, teacher leaders should diagnose the political landscape. The first step in building a "political map" involves discerning who the key players are. One method for identifying key players is the creation of a "power grid." Because of the difficulty associated with accurately identifying certain aspects of political power, this power grid is best viewed as a clarifying tool rather than a precise depiction of the situation.

To create a power grid, draw a table consisting of four boxes. The vertical axis indicates the level of position in the organization. The horizontal axis represents the degree of influence a person has in the organization. One box in each axis will be labeled low and the other will be labeled high.

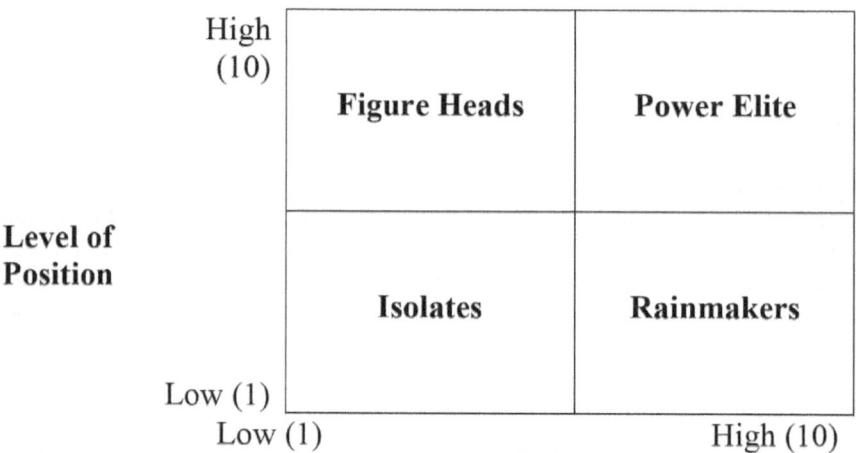

Figure 4.1   Power Grid.

The level of position in the organization is fairly easy to rate. It simply is a reflection of the individual's position on the organizational chart. However, the level of influence is much more subjective to determine.

Determining a person's level of influence requires the informal assessment of two factors. The first factor is the person's network. To determine the strength of a person's network requires information about how many people the person knows and who they interact with regularly. Those with many connections within and outside of the organization have a strong network.

The second factor is credibility. Determining this involves asking the question, "How highly is this person's opinion regarded (regardless of accuracy)?" Someone whose advice or opinion is highly regarded has a high level of credibility. Anyone with a strong network and high credibility is a person with a high level of influence.

Assigning each person relevant to any situation a rating using the scale from 1 (lowest) to 10 (highest) on both their position level and level of influence will provide you with their "power score." This power score can be plotted by finding the point where the two ratings intersect on the matrix. In general, organizational members can be categorized as follows:

- **Rainmakers**—Not in high-level positions, but able to influence the views of many. Some rainmakers have no aspiration to obtain formal authority positions. Others are emerging power players.
- **Power Elite**—Have both high-level positions and the ability to influence the views of many.
- **Isolates**—Low-level positional authority and little influence on others.
- **Figure Heads**—High-level positional authority with very little ability to influence others.

Knowing who the rainmakers and power elite are will help teacher leaders thoughtfully build political leverage. Having strong political leverage is the key to exercising political power.

**Political Leverage.** Political leverage is defined as the ability to get others to do what you want them to do (Mcintyre, 2005). The title of teacher leader may bestow a certain amount of political leverage. However, it is likely that teacher leaders will not yet have the degree of influence required to assume they have the most leverage in a given situation. This is especially true if a teacher leader is hired from outside the organization.

Acquiring political leverage requires boosting one's degree of influence. Boosting one's degree of influence is a process that takes time. However, this process can be accelerated through the use of specific "leverage boosters." One such leverage booster is the power of results.

Delivering results that make your school or district more effective or efficient is very likely to increase the degree of influence. This is especially true if a teacher leader manages to impress those categorized as being among the power elite. For this reason, it is important to clearly understand the goals and expectations of those within this category.

Yet even the most impressive performance has little leverage value if others are not aware of it. This does not mean that the teacher leader needs to act like a showoff or annoy colleagues by bragging. Rather, teacher leaders must strive to do quality work in a way that shapes others' perceptions in a positive direction (McIntyre, 2005).

When it comes to the ability to acquire political leverage, not all projects and assignments are created equal. In fact, for potential influence purposes, all assigned tasks can be categorized by both their importance and visibility. Using visibility and importance as your key dimensions, the following matrix can be used to sort the tasks assigned.

## Project Matrix

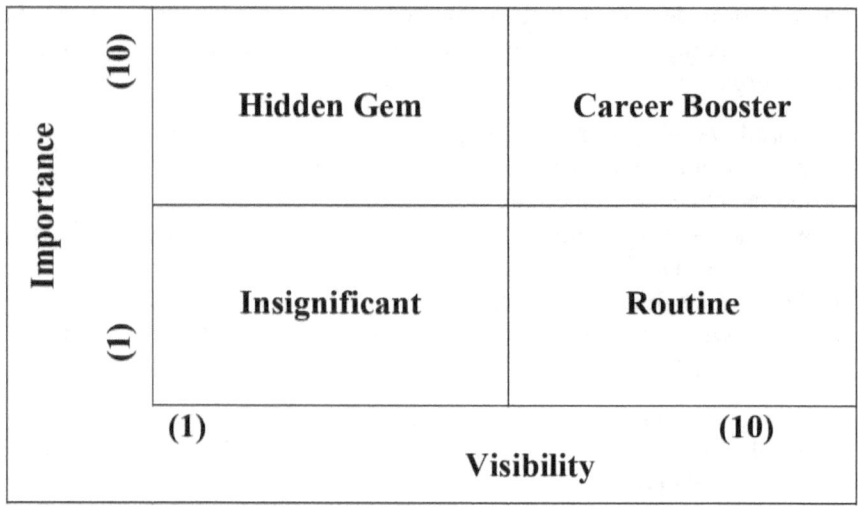

Figure 4.2   Project Matrix.

Career boosters are those projects which are both highly important and highly visible. In a district struggling to lower the special education classification rate, a proposal and presentation designed to address this problem is a potential career booster. It is critical for leverage building that teacher leaders make sure these assignments are completed with high levels of accuracy and quality.

Also highly visible, but unimportant, are projects labeled as "routine." Mandated reports and plans that do not influence actions are examples of routine projects. These assignments need to be completed well enough to avoid attracting any negative attention.

Hidden gems are those projects which are low in visibility but high in importance. Reviewing and revising a poorly designed school crisis plan that has been ignored for an extended period of time is an example of a hidden gem. The goal with hidden gem projects is to bring them out of the darkness and into the spotlight.

If the task is truly significant for the improvement of the school or district, a teacher leader can and should find legitimate means for increasing its prominence. However, since they will be drawing attention to these tasks, it is vital that these tasks are done with great care.

Insignificant projects are neither visible nor important. If a project falls into this category, the teacher leader should do the minimum amount required to complete it. In addition to the power of results, another leverage booster is the power of networks.

Those with political leverage develop and maintain helpful connections with as many people as possible. Teacher leaders must be boundary spanners and networkers who work within and across boundaries and structures to establish social linkages and networks among their peers and within the community (York-Barr & Duke, 2004). Having a strong network of connections is politically important for two reasons.

The first reason is that a network including individuals located at the center of communication networks provides teacher leaders with valuable information. Many times, this information relates to the points of view various individuals and groups have on issues of concern.

Being prepared with information about the points of view held by different interest groups as well as the basis for their positions assists when attempting to negotiate or predict responses to various initiatives. Those identified as rainmakers on a political map are especially valuable sources of information and therefore should be consciously targeted for inclusion in the teacher leader's network.

Second, a network provides teacher leaders with protection against adversaries. More specifically, individuals within a network can provide teacher leaders with advance warnings concerning the actions of underhanded rivals. Additionally, allies in a network will protect the teacher leader by sticking up for them when others attempt to disparage their reputation.

While the identified rainmakers can be important for advance warning, those identified as being among the power elite are vital for protecting a teacher leader's reputation. For this reason, it is vital for teacher leaders to consciously identify and then strive to include those among the power elite within their network.

Building a network requires disciplining oneself to invest in building relationship capital with people you anticipate needing to work with at a later date (Watkins, 2003). It is necessary to devote a good deal of time to working the network of teachers, counselors, administrators, and parents. In order to achieve change, coalition building is often necessary (Gabriel, 2005). The wrong time to attempt to build a network is the moment when one is needed to promote an idea or a goal. Thus, from the earliest part of their tenure teacher leaders must begin the process of constructing a network of powerful allies and connected colleagues.

One method of building relationship capital is through the use of the "chit system." All organizations operate with some form of this system. In a chit system, chits are the unofficial credits which can be cashed in to obtain influence.

Chits can be earned in different ways. In functional organizations, the primary method for earning chits is through exemplary performance. In dysfunctional organizations, personal favors for other organizational members are the dominant means for earning chits.

Regardless of how they are earned, politically savvy teacher leaders build up their bank of chits within the system. At all times there is a debit and credit balance of chits throughout the organization (DeLuca, 1999). Once all of an individual's chits have been spent, their ability to influence others through the use of leverage declines dramatically. Thus, chits must only be spent when it is absolutely necessary for the achievement of political leverage.

Sometimes a teacher leader will need to turn down a request for support made by a colleague. For example, a teacher leader might assess a request and come to the conclusion that by supporting a colleague, they will be damaging their relationship with several key political players. Should this happen, teacher leaders must try to avoid burning bridges.

Avoiding burning bridges requires demonstrating careful consideration of a colleague's appeal. Furthermore, the teacher leader must graciously decline support, placing emphasis on the temporary nature of the denial. Ensure the requesting colleague is aware of the fact that the teacher leader will be willing to provide support if circumstances change. Regardless of your decision, treat everyone with courtesy and respect. Word travels fast and the grapevine can become awfully thorny (Brandon & Seldman, 2004).

A third method used to boost political leverage is the development and maintenance of one's reputation. Because of the importance of a teacher leader's reputation, they must plan their actions carefully and remain sensitive to appearances. This is especially true in the early stages of their tenure in a new position or a new organization (Pfeffer, 1992). Reputation is strongly affected by first impressions. Thus, it is important to develop a good track record from the beginning.

In large part, reputation is determined by how effective someone has been in getting results in their current and previous positions. Those with a solid track record have a reputation that will boost their political leverage. As a result of their solid track record, these individuals are far less likely to be challenged when they attempt to exercise their influence (Pfeffer, 1992).

On the other hand, being on the losing side of issues, particularly if it happens frequently, bestows the reputation of being a loser. Obviously, such an image is quite inconsistent with attaining leverage.

If a teacher leader disagrees with someone that has greater leverage than they do, they should acknowledge their differences on the issue and then state a reasonable basis for their opinion. After stating the basis for their opinion, the teacher leader should agree to go along with the opinion of the more politically powerful person. Viewed from a political perspective, it is important to avoid fighting battles that you cannot win. Instead, make the best of the situation by earning points for being a cooperative team player.

Because reputation is strongly related to one's ability to exercise influence, it must be vigilantly maintained. Teacher leaders must be active in shaping the message they want delivered about them and their work. Without being too obvious, teacher leaders should plant seeds that generate a positive impression. More specifically, teacher leaders should use conversations with rainmakers to subtly, but intentionally, start new positive gossip about their work.

For example, over lunch a teacher leader can share a true anecdote with an influential organizational member highlighting behavior they want others to associate with their image. Perhaps the teacher leader wants to be perceived as being a caring leader. To influence development of this image, the teacher leader can share an anecdote describing how they were late to a meeting with their supervisor because they needed to finish a conversation with a staff member experiencing difficult personal issues. Without stating that they are a caring leader, they are providing rainmakers with the opportunity to reach and then share that conclusion on their own.

If a teacher leader develops a suspicion that a saboteur will slander them by going behind their back to someone in power, they should get there first. By proactively sharing their concern and viewpoint, they frame how the saboteur's message will be perceived. As a consequence of getting there first, the saboteur's message is frequently discredited and they are viewed as acting unprofessionally.

The final leverage booster is the power of knowledge. More specifically, teacher leaders must learn what is important to the power players and then demonstrate the ability to speak their language. When the opportunity arises, teacher leaders must show that they are knowledgeable on issues that are of concern to the power players.

One opportunity to demonstrate this knowledge is meetings. When power players are members of a meeting, teacher leaders must prepare in advance. If possible, they should ascertain the meeting agenda. Using their knowledge and network, teacher leaders can ascertain the formal and informal priorities each power player has on each of the agenda topics. Then they can thoroughly prepare so that they arrive at the meeting with a strong, carefully thought-out point of view on the topics. This will lead power players to view the teacher leader as a source of information and a potentially valuable resource.

**Political Adversaries.** Whereas supporters and allies increase leverage, political adversaries reduce it. While it is desirable and important to avoid creating political adversaries, it is not always feasible. Sometimes adversaries have motives that seem counterproductive or even incomprehensible. When this happens, it is valuable to examine the person's motives in an attempt to determine the underlying reasons motivating the behavior.

Focused adversaries comprise one category of political enemies. These individuals are motivated to achieve their goals and view the teacher leader as a potential obstacle. Their actions often create ongoing power struggles that inevitably result in someone losing. If the loser is the focused adversary, then they may become stealth opponents, retaliating in quietly lethal ways.

The better approach for dealing with focused adversaries is converting them to allies. This conversion begins with the adversary believing the teacher leader understands their concerns. In addition, the adversary must be convinced that the teacher leader is not an obstacle to the achievement of their goals. Instead, the teacher leader wants them to see how working together will contribute to their success. If they believe that working with the teacher leader presents an opportunity to shine, then they are on the path toward becoming an ally.

Occasionally a focused adversary will not convert. Should this happen, the best approach is containment. To contain an uncooperative focused adversary requires increasing political leverage. Most often, this means enlisting the support of organizational members that have greater power and influence.

Suppose a colleague wants to block the teacher leader's initiative to promote cross-curricular emphasis on developing higher-level thinking skills. The teacher leader has unsuccessfully attempted to convince their adversary of the benefits of cooperating on this initiative. To keep them from successfully blocking the initiative, the teacher leader reaches out to the principal to make sure they understand and support the initiative. Now that the teacher leader has obtained the principal's support, the focused adversary will need to contain their hostility and grudgingly participate in the initiative.

A second category of political enemies is comprised of the emotional adversary. This adversary is truly out of control, driven by intense emotional needs (McIntyre, 2005). Emotional adversaries are easily identified because they create problems for everyone, not just the teacher leader.

Dealing with an emotional adversary requires self-control. Remember, their behavior is triggered by their needs, not someone's actions. An emotional response on the part of the teacher leader is exactly the reward this category of adversary is seeking. The teacher leader can control reactions by maintaining a calm, rational demeanor at all times. Because the reward being sought will not be provided, this adversary will eventually reduce their level of disruptive behavior in the teacher leader's presence.

The final category of political enemies is the vengeful adversary. This adversary is unmistakably out to get the teacher leader personally. Sometimes, they make it is obvious that they do not care for the teacher leader. Other times, they act as stealthy opponents, avoiding direct confrontation.

Usually, the vengeful adversary is retaliating for something the teacher leader has done. Therefore, to convert these adversaries requires examination of what might have been done to create their resentment. If the teacher leader has wronged the person and the adversary is somewhat reasonable, they can apologize for their actions and make the appropriate amends.

If the person is unreasonable, the teacher leader must strive for containment. In other words, the focus shifts to protecting oneself against any further damage. In a professional manner, the teacher leader should alert their direct supervisor of the problem and describe the actions they have taken to reach a resolution. This is likely to ensure that future attacks are perceived as being personal and not professional in nature. Thus, the attacks will lose credibility.

Politics are a fact of life associated with organizations. If teacher leaders ignore this fact or attempt to avoid engaging in politics, they will simply create opportunities for the less squeamish to dominate the game. As a consequence of inaction, both those they lead and the teacher leader's career will suffer.

**School Culture.** In chapter 2, it was stated that every school has a distinct culture that serves to shapes its members' beliefs and behavior. The focus in that chapter was on the relationship between school culture and the potential effectiveness of teacher leadership. The focus of this section is on how a teacher leader can assess and shape school culture to promote student achievement.

Some cultures support the school's mission and purpose. Other cultures are so toxic they derail the organization's efforts to improve or reform. Therefore, one of the goals for any teacher leader is developing an understanding of the culture of their work unit and of the larger organization. To develop this understanding requires knowledge of the elements of school culture.

At the core of a school's culture is its mission and purpose (Deal & Peterson, 1999). Put simply, mission and purpose serve as the focal points for what people do. This is not to be confused with mission statements. Whereas some mission statements are living documents, most are wall decorations which are either poorly communicated or ignored.

To understand the real mission and purpose of an organization, one must delve into its values, beliefs, and norms. Values are the standards set for what defines excellence. In some schools, extracurricular success is valued above all else. In others, it is learning for the elite as demonstrated by acceptance into prestigious colleges. Values are the core of what the organization considers important (Peterson & Deal, 2002).

Beliefs are the organizational members' cognitive views about truth and reality. These views represent core understandings about major aspects of the organization. More specifically, beliefs determine views of such areas as teacher responsibility for student learning, parents' capabilities to provide a home environment conducive to learning, and student capacity for learning.

Norms are the unstated, shared rules guiding organizational members' behavior. In organizations, these norms include expectations for how one will dress and behave. For example, in one school the norm may be to use preparation periods for the planning of instruction or the assessment of student work. In another school, the norm may be to use preparation periods for reading the newspaper or making personal phone calls. Violating the norm in either situation is likely to result in the provisions of sanctions by other organizational members.

Rituals, ceremonies, and traditions are the expression of culture. Rituals are procedures or routines that have been infused with deeper meaning (Peterson & Deal, 2002). More than just technical actions, rituals connect common experiences with the organization's deeper values. For example, at a staff member orientation, veteran staff members voluntarily come to the luncheon to welcome new staff. This act is an expression of the school's deeper value of being a welcoming, professional learning community.

Ceremonies are periodic communal events designed to celebrate successes and recognize special contributions. Examples of ceremonies include award banquets, assemblies, and retirement dinners.

Like ceremonies, traditions are significant events with special meaning. Traditions occur with regularity throughout the course of a year. Traditions and ceremonies differ because traditions do not need to be large communal events. Examples of traditions include "dress down Fridays" and giving flowers or providing food for colleagues that are ill.

Past events influence present cultural practices in dramatic ways. Knowledge of the history of an organization is critical to developing a deeper understanding of the culture of that organization. For this reason, teacher leaders need to develop an in-depth understanding of the history of their unit as well as the history of the larger organization.

The final element of organizational culture is symbols. Symbols concretely represent organizational beliefs and values. More specifically, they represent organizational members' hopes and priorities. For example, a school valuing students' postgraduation contributions maintains a wall of fame in its vestibule. A school that values the status associated with the organizational hierarchy has reserved parking closest to the school building for administrative staff members.

**Importance of Culture.** Organizational culture influences and shapes staff members' focus, commitment, motivation, and productivity. In other words, the culture of the organization has a large role in determining how teachers, students, and administrators think, act, and feel. Official policies and regulations prescribe how administration thinks things should be done, but culture determines what actually happens.

When culture does not support change initiatives, improvement does not occur (Deal & Peterson, 1999). More specifically, if the values, beliefs, and norms remain constant—even when structures and procedures are changed—organizations quickly return to the status quo.

For these reasons, as a teacher leader one of the priorities is the assessment of culture. More specifically, teacher leaders must attempt to determine those aspects of the culture enabling high performance and those aspects serving as a barrier to effective performance.

Assessment of the culture of an organization is a prerequisite to cultural change. Attempting to change the culture prior to developing a thorough understanding of it is almost guaranteed to result in failure. Yet, this assessment is not without risks.

Two types of risks exist when assessing organizational culture. First, because of the complexity involved with assessing something as abstract as culture, it is possible the assessment could be inaccurate. Second, because of the ingrained nature of most school cultures, the organization may not be ready to receive feedback.

Because of these risks, a teacher leader must be careful when assessing the culture of his or her organization. The next section presents strategies designed to improve the accuracy of a cultural assessment.

**Assessing Culture.** The culture of any organization will fall somewhere along a continuum from weak to strong. Weak cultures invite leaders to take strong actions. The members of weak cultures are hoping for change. Strong cultures are the opposite. A strong culture will resist change. Furthermore, members of a strong culture will reject newcomers they perceive to be the enemies of tradition.

A second dimension the culture of any organization will vary on is the degree to which it is negative or positive. A negative culture is characterized by the need to blame, an overall defeatist attitude, and pessimistic beliefs about the growth potential of staff and students. The mission of the members in a negative culture is to preserve or improve the outcomes for the adults in the school.

Just the opposite, a positive culture focuses on student and teacher learning. To achieve this mission, members of a positive culture work collegially as they strive to continuously improve their practice. Members in these cultures share responsibility for student outcomes and hold a set of optimistic beliefs about the potential of both staff and students. The key to determining the type of culture is to conduct a thoughtful, systematic assessment of both past and present actions.

The assessment of the culture begins with an understanding of the organization's history. The culture of any organization has been molded over time as members have dealt with critical incidents, emotional events, and major accomplishments. Values and beliefs have been shaped by experience and then cemented by use and reinforcement. The critical question a teacher leader must seek to answer about the history is, "What forces have pushed this school's culture in one direction or another?"

One strategy for answering this question is through the development of a visual history. While this task can be done by oneself or in a small group, it is far more effective when all staff members are involved in the process. In fact, this is an excellent activity for a staff meeting. Doing this activity demonstrates a desire to understand and respect the history of the group.

If the decision is made to involve the staff in creating the visual history, then divide them into small groups by the decades in which they joined the organization. Provide each group with a piece of chart paper and a marker. Direct them to brainstorm the major events which occurred in the school or district during those years. Points each group should consider include:

- Who were the formal and informal leaders?
- What crises and controversies occurred and how were they dealt with?
- What major accomplishments were achieved?
- What major changes were implemented?
- What were the common characteristics of students and the community?

Once the groups have completed their charts, starting with the earliest decade, have a spokesperson from each group tell the story of that decade. As each group's spokesperson shares the description of their decade, the teacher leader should listen for those events and people that have shaped the culture into what it is today.

Equipped with a better understanding of the organization's history, a teacher leader can now begin their assessment of the core aspects of the current culture. This assessment is an attempt to uncover the genuine mission and purpose of the organization. While it is difficult to uncover these often-hidden aspects of culture, there are several cultural elements that can be examined in order to identify them.

One item that should not be relied upon exclusively is the organization's formal mission statement. Formal mission statements should not be viewed as defining the purpose of the organization. At best, they represent those aspects of the culture leaders find useful to publish as an ideology or focus (Schein, 2004).

To unveil the authentic mission and purpose requires observing and interpreting visible aspects of the culture. One such aspect of any culture is the rituals engaged in by staff members. Determining which rituals staff members engage in and what these rituals communicate is important to understanding commonly held core values and beliefs. Examples of the rituals that could be examined include:

- how new teachers are introduced to the faculty,
- how new students and their parents are welcomed,
- how the school year begins and ends,
- how teachers are recognized for earning tenure or retiring.

Similarly, it is valuable to examine the ceremonies which occur over the course of the year. More specifically, what ceremonies occur and what do they recognize? Some of the ceremonies that could be examined include:

- opening/ending of school ceremonies,
- seasonal ceremonies (women's history month, Halloween, etc.),
- student/staff recognition ceremonies,
- homecoming ceremonies.

Another visible aspect of the culture which will provide clues to the genuine mission and purpose is the organization's core symbols. Like traditions, rituals, and ceremonies, core symbols represent the values and beliefs held by the organization's members. A teacher leader must attempt to determine the meaning of the symbols found throughout the organization. Some of the items to examine include

- logos/mottos,
- banners and posters,
- displays of student work,
- displays of past achievements,
- halls of honor, and
- pictures of current or past students or staff members.

As teacher leaders examine these symbols, they should ask themselves what messages are communicated. By doing this, the teacher leader will be one step closer to understanding the values and beliefs held by the members of the organization.

**Shaping the Culture.** Having both conducted an assessment of the organization's history and interpreted the visible aspects of the culture, teacher leaders are now prepared to synthesize what they have learned. The goal when completing this synthesis is the identification of the cultural elements supporting effective performance. These are the cultural aspects that must be praised and reinforced. A second goal is the identification of the cultural elements that are impeding performance. Teacher leaders must help reshape these elements so that they support the results desired.

The following matrix uses the dimensions previously described to categorize the major needs of each type of organizational culture.

| | Negative | Positive |
|---|---|---|
| **Strong** | Transformation | Sustaining Success |
| **Weak** | Turnaround | Realignment |

Figure 4.3   Culture.

By far the most challenging culture for any instructional leader is one requiring a transformation. These cultures are firmly entrenched and toxic. In this type of culture, there are few, if any, collectively held values, beliefs, or norms promoting student achievement.

If you are a teacher leader in an organization with a culture that requires a transformation, you will need patience, persistence, and outside support. Chances are that this type of culture has developed over an extended period of time, so do not expect it to change quickly.

Attempting to transform a negative culture is a very risky business. Those that have benefited from the status quo will resist and reject these efforts. Teacher leaders as cultural change agents in this situation are likely to be attacked both personally and professionally. These attacks may be overt and obvious or covert and deceptive.

To survive these attacks requires strong alliances with your colleagues and your direct supervisor. Not only will they "have your back," they will be able to support you. More specifically, through listening to your concerns, these individuals will offer hope and healing during what is likely to be a difficult period of time.

In contrast to the culture requiring transformation is one that requires sustaining success. This type of culture is both strong and supportive. In other words, the collectively shared values, beliefs, and norms of staff members support the attainment of the organization's goals.

When working with a culture that requires sustaining success, emphasis must be placed on understanding and being accepted by the members of that culture. Staff members in this type of culture want reassurance that no one will attempt to radically change the positive culture they have developed.

The good news is that a teacher leader will very likely have the time required to achieve this learning. When dealing with a culture that requires sustaining success, there will most likely be no need for urgent, early action.

Cultures requiring a turnaround do not support the organization's goals. However, the negative norms, values, and beliefs prevalent in this culture are weak. Many of the staff members in this type of culture recognize the need for a change. Oftentimes, the staff members working in these cultures feel demoralized and hopeless.

When the cultural assessment reveals the need for a turnaround, action by leadership is both expected and necessary. This action must include leaders recognizing, celebrating, and reinforcing those cultural elements which are positive.

If hope is to be restored, then positive values, beliefs, and norms must be regularly and publicly recognized. This may require designing and implementing new ceremonies or eliminating dying or negative ones. Furthermore, because of the feelings of hopelessness that exist, it will take persistence and time to develop strong positive cultural norms.

On the other hand, this recognition of positive cultural elements must be balanced with open recognition of past problems. Failure to do this is likely to lead others to conclude that leaders do not understand the reality of the current situation.

In order to limit varying perceptions of what is being said, the sharing of feedback is best done in a whole group setting, such as a faculty meeting. When leaders provide this feedback, they must strive to be direct, nonjudgmental, and specific. Above all else, leaders must avoid placing blame. While tempting, blaming is exactly the type of negative behavior leaders are striving to eliminate.

A culture that requires realignment also demands that leaders take action. However, the focus of this action is different. In this case, the culture does have positive elements, but they are not firmly established. Because the positive aspects of the culture are not deeply ingrained, a negative event could easily lead this culture to become one requiring a turnaround.

The most important role for the leaders of a culture requiring realignment is strengthening the existing positive aspects of the culture. Leaders must strive to make them become both deeply ingrained and collectively held. Oftentimes this can be achieved through revising the actions conducted during regular events into ones which meaningfully reinforce desired core values.

For example, faculty meetings are frequently dreaded administrative events (Jennings, 2007). They can become gatherings in which relationships are built, problems are solved, decisions are made, and professional growth occurs. Doing this would reinforce the desired core values of professionalism and collegiality.

School assemblies can become opportunities for staff and students to build connections and share school pride. This would reinforce the importance of positive, respectful relationships between staff and students as well as the belief that being a student or staff member in this school is special.

At the end of the year, staff members could come together to celebrate successes and grieve endings. This would communicate acknowledgment of achievement while at the same time allowing for closure.

All of these changes and others specific to a situation will result in strengthening the positive aspects of the current culture. The key is to determine which activities are not currently reinforcing the positive cultural aspects. Once identified, the activities should be revised so they support and reinforce the cultural aspects the leaders want to solidify.

Culture is to a group what personality is to an individual. It is constantly being enacted and created by interactions with others. Yet, there are prevailing values, beliefs, and norms that serve to guide or constrain behavior.

The organization's culture shapes the way staff and students think, feel, and act. Thus, as a teacher leader, demonstrating the ability to assess, diagnose, and shape the culture you are expected to be part of leading is critical to your success.

This chapter has focused on assessing and then subsequently using that understanding of school culture and politics to achieve desired results. Consistent and ethical use of school culture and politics to positively influence school climate and achieve desired outcomes is an essential part of teacher leadership. Chapter 5 focuses on another important part of teacher leadership, promoting the professional growth of colleagues.

*Chapter 5*

# Promoting Professional Growth

Teacher leaders are commonly tasked with providing professional learning opportunities to colleagues. The common assumption is that experience as an effective classroom teacher is sufficient preparation for teaching adults. However, assuming that teaching children and teaching adults is the same is incorrect. Adults have unique learning needs, and teachers are frequently a more difficult audience to work with than students.

If teacher leaders are to provide meaningful professional learning opportunities, they must develop a new body of knowledge and skills. More specifically, teacher leaders must develop understanding of the characteristics of adult learners, as well as how to manage the process of change. In addition, teacher leaders must learn how to prepare and deliver staff training sessions. Developing this knowledge and skillset is the subject of this chapter.

**Characteristics of Adult Learners.** Effective teacher leaders must hold an accurate understanding of adult learning (Tomal et al., 2014). The first characteristic of adult learners that a teacher leader must remember is that participating teachers have a wealth of prior knowledge they can use as a resource to support current learning. If activated, this prior knowledge can facilitate understanding of the new knowledge and assist in establishing neural connections that lead to long-term retention.

Additionally, demonstrating a lack of respect for the experience and knowledge of an audience of teachers is likely to be considered offensive. Professional learning opportunity participants will not learn from a teacher leader they perceive as disrespectful. Thus, to be effective in their role as a staff development provider, teacher leaders must acknowledge and make use of participating teachers' prior knowledge and experiences. This can be done by asking participants to share what they already know, providing time for participants to share examples and experiences, and explicitly acknowledging participants' current levels of expertise.

Unfortunately, past experiences can also serve as a significant barrier to effectively working with adult learners. Past experiences may have resulted in the development of preconceived biases and ideas about the topic being presented. For example, a teacher that states "computer-assisted instruction is just the district's attempt to reduce the number of staff" is highly unlikely to be an engaged, positive workshop participant, at least on this topic.

Additionally, teachers who have experienced initiative upon initiative without ever having a sustained focus will likely express cynicism toward new ideas. The attitude of "this too shall pass," or "this is just this year's new thing," makes it difficult for audience participants to invest time and effort into learning something new. For this reason, it is essential that those providing professional learning opportunities communicate the personal value of the content early and often.

The second characteristic of adult learners is that they have the overarching goal of learning relevant information that has practical applications to solving real-world problems. Adult learners approach professional learning opportunities with the desire to learn how the information shared can be used, preferably as soon as possible. The effective teacher leader ensures that all participating teachers are provided with ideas they can apply to their own situation. Also, participating teachers must be given ample opportunities to engage in activities that encourage them to connect new information to their own classrooms.

Connected to this desire for practical application is adult learners' need to know why they are learning something. Effective teacher leaders provide participants with reasons for why they are expected to learn something new. They also clarify expectations for what will improve as a result of acquiring this new knowledge and skill set.

In comparison to children, adult learners are more self-directed in their learning. As a result, the third characteristic of adult learners that teacher leaders must be cognizant of is that they require some degree of control over their learning. To meet this need, teacher leaders should provide participants with appropriate choices as well as self-assessment activities. Choice is particularly important for providing adults with opportunities that appeal to various learning modalities.

**Understanding Change.** For professional learning activities to be effective, they must result in positive changes to instructional practices. The ultimate goal of professional learning is improved student achievement. Sometimes, the required changes are incremental and can be characterized as an extension of how things are already done. Incremental changes are usually not met with strong reactions from staff.

However, when new practices require changes in beliefs and/or culture, they are likely to be far more disruptive. Changes to how things are normally done are far more likely to elicit strong emotional reactions from staff. Individuals' reactions to proposed change will depend upon how they perceive it. Is the change more likely to result in loss or growth? When the answer is loss, people may demonstrate resistance through a variety of difficult behaviors. This is even the case when the changes are necessary and logical.

Underlying the resistance to change is fear. More specifically, difficult behaviors expressed by staff members are commonly an expression of two sources of fear. First, staff members fear the change will result in unacceptable loss. Having worked hard at what they are currently doing, they do not want to change.

In addition, a call to change can be equated to an accusation that what is currently being done is somehow wrong. Some staff members may feel that if a teacher leader shares content they do not know, it will demonstrate the inadequacy of that staff member's knowledge and skills. Staff members do not want to lose their perceived sense of competence.

Second, staff members may fear that they will not have or be able to develop the skills needed to succeed with a new initiative. Perhaps they do not have the time required to invest in making the change, or they are filled with fear of risk of failure.

Regardless of the reason for resistance, the bottom line is that teachers' initial concern with change is that it will not be good for them. Typically, initial resistance is not the result of concern for how the change will negatively impact the students (Gabriel, 2005).

Many potentially positive initiatives have been derailed by staff opposition. Part of the reason for this is that opposition to change can spread like a virus. The irrational fears of a few can quickly be transformed into mob rule (Reeves, 2009). An effective teacher leader knows how to manage the process of change.

**Change Management.** The difficult behaviors that emerge during the change process are predictable and inevitable, but they can be managed. In fact, if your proposal does not engender some opposition, the question becomes: Is what you are proposing truly meaningful change? There are three actions a teacher leader can take that will reduce resistance to change initiatives.

First, teacher leaders must be careful with how the change is presented. When introducing a change to current practice, the effective teacher leader will "frame" it in a way that affirms the professional and personal worth of all those involved. Asking teachers to share the work they are currently engaging in, validating this work, and then asking them to consider how the new ideas might fit in with the excellent repertoire they are already using is an effective approach. In addition, teacher leaders increase collegial engagement when they frame the approach as adaptable and flexible (Margolis, 2009).

Successful framing of proposed changes places the new desired behaviors into perspective by identifying what will not change (Reeves, 2009). Clearly articulating values, practices, traditions, and relationships that will be maintained places the change in the context of stability. An example of how this might sound is, "Before we discuss the implementation of editing and revision checklists for writing, let's start with some assurances. We will still use the writing process during our dedicated writing workshop time. In addition, we will continue to use the common writing rubrics for assessment developed by each grade-level team. We continue to value the work you have completed up to this point and that will not change."

Furthermore, presenting the change as a modification to current practice keeps it from becoming a pervasive and overwhelming threat. The successful teacher leader communicates the message that "you, and our work together for our students, are so precious that we have a shared responsibility to be the best we can," not, "you are broken and I am here to fix you."

When change is framed as a meaningful opportunity within the context of stability, the odds in favor of successful implementation are increased dramatically. Framing a change in this manner will not eliminate the cynicism of skeptics, but it will provide the teacher leader with the space and time needed to gain trust (Reeves, 2009).

Which must change first in order for staff to "buy-in" to a new initiative, attitudes or behaviors? It turns out that change leaders do not gain commitment to changes through inspiration, demands, pleading, or seminars. Instead, commitment comes from attaining results that show the effect of the change is in the best interest of teachers and students. Thus, the second action teacher leaders must take to reduce staff resistance is to focus on changing behavior, not attitudes. If you get staff members to implement change and, as a result, they see improved outcomes, then eventually their attitude toward the change will become more favorable.

Because implementation precedes commitment, the majority of time spent during professional learning opportunities should focus on participants practicing small pieces of knowledge and skills that are easy to implement. It is worthwhile to spend some time providing the rationale for, as well as the value of, the change. However, in order to change behavior, not attitudes, this should be a small percentage of the time.

The third action a teacher leader can take to reduce resistance to change is to make sure there are opportunities for effective and repeated practice of the desired professional behavior. Beyond the initial professional learning activities, staff members must apply the new knowledge and skills in their own context and achieve short-term wins. Effective short-term wins are based on application objectives that are meaningful and attainable.

In addition, quality feedback must be provided in order to reinforce effective practice while modifying ineffective practice. As an activity designed to give meaningful feedback to students and teachers and to improve professional practice, formative assessments are an important means of recognizing short-term wins. Regardless of how they are achieved, without short-term wins the pain associated with change will overwhelm the anticipated long-term benefits (Reeves, 2009).

Despite taking these three actions, the short-term popularity of changes will likely be low. Changes inevitably represent risk, loss, and fear, a combination of factors that does not typically result in high favorability. This is compounded by the phenomenon that things often get worse before they get better. As staff experience an innovation requiring new skills and understandings, their performance and confidence typically dips (Fullan, 2007).

Teacher leaders must be prepared to stand up for initially unpopular yet potentially effective practices. In addition, they must provide support and encouragement to colleagues during the implementation dip. High-impact teacher leaders emphasize the potential effectiveness of instructional changes over their initial popularity and implementation challenges.

**Workshop Planning.** There are many ways to engage teachers in professional learning. One commonly used method is the traditional workshop session. Well-run workshops have value for participants. Depending on the content, workshop participants can learn new ideas and skills, work with others to construct meaning, and be exposed to different ways of thinking. Regardless of the content, structure, or format, effective workshops require advanced planning.

Workshop planning can be divided into long-range and short-term tasks. The first task a teacher leader assigned to conduct a workshop must do is to assess his or her own knowledge of the topic. If the teacher leader doesn't have the expertise required to conduct a workshop on the topic, they must do the work necessary to acquire it. Commonly, teachers already question the premise that a peer could possess expert knowledge. If workshop participants sense a teacher leader does not know the subject matter, they are likely to demonstrate disruptive behavior. The type of disruption can range from outright challenges of credibility to ignoring the presentation while doing other work.

This is not to be confused with the misconception that as a staff developer, the teacher leader must know everything. In fact, when teacher leaders explained how they worked through using a new approach with their students and admitted their own struggles openly, colleagues were more open to new approaches (Margolis, 2009). Acting as if one knows all the answers frequently leads to rambling, incorrect answers, and poor explanations. Incorrect answers and explanations ultimately damage credibility and can lead workshop participants to take actions that are ineffective.

It is alright not to know the answer to some of the participants' questions. If a participant asks a question that the teacher leader does not know the answer to, they can respond by saying so. In addition, they can assure the person asking the question that they will seek out the answer and provide it to them as soon as possible. If this is done infrequently, it will not damage the presenter's credibility.

**Audience Background.** After assessing their own current knowledge, teacher leaders charged with presenting a workshop must assess the knowledge and interests of the participants. The following is a series of questions a teacher leader can ask the workshop sponsor to determine the audience's background:

- What are the job titles and roles of the participants?
- Have they had any previous training in this subject?
- What, if any, expectations for the outcomes of this training have been communicated to participants?
- What brings these people to the workshop? Is it required or did they choose to attend?
- What kind, if any, of follow-up to this workshop has been planned?
- What, if anything, have participants already been told about the format and content of the workshop?

Another way to gather information from future workshop participants is to survey them prior to planning content. The following three questions are especially valuable for gathering information in advance:

- What do you already know about this subject?
- Specifically, what do you want to learn about this topic?
- What do we need to accomplish for this workshop to be effective?

Finding out what people already know, as well as what they want to know, makes it possible to tailor the content of a presentation to the interests and needs of the audience. Having gathered, organized, and reviewed information from future workshop participants, it is time to prepare the content of the presentation.

**Workshop Content.** When planning the content for a workshop, the teacher leader must conduct a thoughtful analysis of the purpose and desired outcomes for their presentation. The purpose of the workshop refers to the depth of ability participants should attain as a result of the training.

If the presentation is intended to promote awareness of a topic, then the presentation should place more emphasis on content than processing and practice. However, if the goal is the development of a new skill, then the balance between the presentation of content and opportunities for practice should be roughly divided evenly. If the goal is for participants to transfer the presented training concepts to their own classroom then the emphasis must be placed on practice and processing rather than content.

The desired outcomes are stated as broad training goals. It is important to remember that improved student achievement is the ultimate purpose for providing any staff training. Thus, goal statements can't simply focus on what the teacher will learn and do differently as a result of the learning experience. Instead, outcome statements must include what the results will be for students.

For example, *"teachers will demonstrate* the knowledge and skill required to instruct students on how to generate an academic argument *so that students will receive proficient scores on the district's argumentation writing rubric."* The length of training time available and the purpose for the training will determine the number of possible training goals.

Broad training goals must be further broken down into objectives. The content of the objectives is the knowledge and skills required to meet the goal(s). For example, the aforementioned goal can be broken down into the following objectives: Teachers will understand and be able to teach students how to

- generate a claim statement,
- generate grounds to support a claim statement,
- generate backing to support a claim statement,
- provide appropriate qualifiers as part of a claim.

Many times, objectives need to be further analyzed in order to determine the specific content for a workshop. For example, one of the above objectives, generating a claim statement, requires teachers to know and be able to do the following (see table 5.1):

Table 5.1 Sample Knowledge and Skills Breakdown

| Knowledge (Teachers Must Know . . .) | Skill (Teachers Must be Able to . . .) |
|---|---|
| Definition of a claim statement. | Teach students to generate a claim statement. |
| Qualities of an effective claim statement. | Teach students to use subordinate clauses to "set up" an argument. |
| Why the claim statement is an essential part of an argument. | |
| Definition of subordinate clauses. | |
| Reasons for using subordinate clauses to set up an argument. | |

Once the sub-objectives are articulated, they can be grouped into meaningful chunks and sequenced into a logical order. Continuing with the example of generating an academic argument, the content for the training outline might look like the following:

- Generating a claim statement
    - Definition and qualities of an effective claim statement.
    - Why a claim statement is an essential part of an argument?
    - Methods for teaching students to generate a claim statement.
    - Definition and reasons for using subordinate clauses to support an argument.
    - Methods for teaching students to use subordinate clauses to set up an argument.

The next step in the planning process is determining how much time is necessary to adequately address each of the identified chunks of information. When making this determination, it is critical to bear in mind that if a teacher leader attempts to present too many ideas at once without giving colleagues time to work with a single idea for a meaningful period of time, their fellow teachers will feel overloaded (Margolis, 2009).

While there is no definitive answer to how many chunks can be taught in an hour, a general guideline is to limit the quantity presented to between two and three chunks per hour of training. Following these guidelines, the objective of generating a claim statement would require approximately two hours of training time.

**Evaluation of Outcomes.** Effective professional learning shouldn't be judged solely by the delivery of the content. A fun, exciting workshop can be a pleasant way to spend an afternoon. However, if participants do not learn and then apply anything of significance, then it was simply a positive social experience. Part of planning for an effective workshop presentation is determining how to assess the learning achieved by the participants.

The common evaluation of a workshop involves distributing and reviewing evaluation forms. The content of these forms is primarily helpful for the improvement of the presentation and for gauging the emotional response to the training experience. The content of evaluation forms neither reveals if participants understood and are prepared to apply the material nor measures student results from classroom application.

During the workshop, the teacher leader must use formative assessment to determine participants' level of understanding. This information makes it possible to adjust the presentation and provide re-teaching if necessary. As part of planning content, the second decision a presenter must make is how they will determine if participants are achieving the desired learning during the workshop.

Determining the impact of the training connects with the student portion of the original desired outcome statement(s). In the example of teaching students to generate academic arguments, the measurement of success identified is proficient scores on district argumentation writing rubrics. If scores on district argumentation writing rubrics are available for the time prior, they can be compared to student scores achieved after conducting the workshop. This pre- to post-comparison serves as a measure of the training's impact.

**Learning Activities.** The next step of workshop planning is matching objectives to activities. In other words, what is the best way to provide the content in order for the learners to develop the appropriate understandings? Typically, content is shared through a combination of verbal explanations followed by processing activities.

Workshop participants can realistically maintain focus on a speaker's verbal message for between seven and ten minutes (Margolis, 2009). Thus, the best presentations provide clear, concise, brief explanations followed by longer periods of practice, application, and debriefing. In addition, the human body was not designed for extended periods of sitting. In order to maximize learning, workshop participants should be up and moving between every thirty and forty-five minutes.

When selecting activities, it is important to make sure they achieve the intended objective. If the goal is to review the content provided, then the activity must require participants to achieve that goal. In addition, aim for variety and, if possible, make the activities fun for the participants. Table 5.2 is an example of the type of grid a teacher leader could use to plan the content of their workshop.

Table 5.2 Sample Workshop Planning Grid

| Content | Formative Assessment | Activity |
|---|---|---|
| *Section One—Generating A Claim Statement* | | |
| Definition and qualities of an effective claim statement. | Explanation in their own words of the definition of a claim statement. | 1. PowerPoint Presentation of definition with examples/non-examples. <br> 2. Think-pair-share—what is a claim statement? <br> 3. Using Smart Board, identify if it is or is not an example of a claim statement. |
| | List of qualities of an effective claim statement. | 1. PowerPoint Presentation of qualities of effective claim statements with models. <br> 2. Choral practice activity. <br> 3. Roundtable activity. |
| Brain Break | | Macarena |

**Designing Visual Aids.** The final step of long-range planning for a workshop is the creation and acquisition of required materials. According to Peoples (1992), workshop participants receive the majority of their information (75 percent) through visuals. Thus, it is important for workshop presenters to develop and use high-quality visual aids.

One type of visual aid that has a significant influence on teachers' willingness to consider new strategies is examples of student work. If appropriate and possible, the teacher leader should share recent student work from his or her own classroom. This action is compelling to teachers as they consider the relative value of a new teaching strategy (Margolis, 2009).

The most common visual aids used when making presentations are computer slideshows, flip charts, and handouts. The following are guidelines for designing each of these visual aids.

Computer slideshows are visual design tools that are both popular and efficient. However, like all presentation tools, when overdone or done poorly these types of presentations lose their effectiveness. In order for computer slideshows to be designed effectively, keep the following guidelines in mind:

- Select a graphic or theme and stick with it throughout the design of the presentation.
- Employ a design template that uses as little of the screen as possible.
- Follow the eight-by-eight rule: use a maximum of eight words across and eight lines down each slide.
- When presenting lists, design the slide so that one line can be revealed at a time.
- To emphasize an item, make it a different color than the rest.
- Headings should be 44-point type, and body text should be between 24- and 32-point type.
- Use one type of transition between slides.
- Limit colors to two per slide (plus black).
- Ensure there is enough contrast between typeface and background. Most audience members prefer a light typeface on a dark background.
- Don't overuse clipart, animations, or sound effects.

Flip charts are often used to record participants' ideas. However, they are occasionally designed in advance for use as a visual aid for a presentation. When designing flip charts as visual aids for presentations, keep the following guidelines in mind:

- Consider boxing or underlining the heading of each chart.
- Decide if you want to leave space to add information during the session.

- Make letters 1 to 3 inches tall. Each inch of height makes it possible to see from 15 feet away. Thus, 1-inch letters can be seen at 15 feet, 2-inch letters can be seen at 30 feet, and so on.
- Have ten lines or fewer per page.
- Trace models or drawings that you like.
- Use color systematically. For example, use dark colors (brown, black, or blue) for words and bright colors for highlighting. Use red and green sparingly; 7 percent of the population is color blind.

Oftentimes, staff members are provided with handouts at workshops. The teacher leader can improve the quality of handouts if he or she considers the following guidelines:

- Choose a strong title.
- Directly relate the handouts to the presentation's key ideas.
- Keep the arrangement of the handouts simple.
- Opt for fewer rather than more pages (ten to twenty pages per day of training).
- Number the pages.
- Include a bibliography of references.
- Recommend appropriate books, websites, videos, and other resources for additional information.

When using handouts, reproduce enough for every member of your intended audience, plus 10 percent, and always bring a copy of the master edition with you to the training.

The day of the workshop, the presenter should strive to arrive early to the workshop location. How early varies based on the type of training and the teacher leader's preferences and needs. Yet, there are always tasks that must be addressed in advance of participants' arrival. At a minimum, the teacher leader should arrive twenty minutes before the workshop is scheduled to begin.

**Physical Environment.** The first task to address is the preparation of the physical environment. Workshop participants are more likely to contribute actively and learn more from the workshop if the physical setting is comfortable and conducive to achieving the session's objectives.

Desirable physical environments will vary depending on the size of the group and the activities planned for the meeting. The following guidelines for the physical environment of the workshop should be considered by the teacher leader:

- The key to seating arrangements is variety and appropriateness. The seating arrangements must be matched to the type of activities that will occur in the session.

- A U-shape or semicircle seating arrangement is best for groups of twelve to twenty-two staff members, and is well-suited to large group discussions.
- A single square or round shape is best for groups of eight to twelve staff members, and is well-suited to problem-solving.
- A V-shape with tables of four to five staff members apiece facing the front of the room is best for groups of sixteen to forty. This arrangement is well-suited to small-group work at each table.
- A traditional arrangement of front-facing rows is appropriate for any size group, and is particularly well-suited to the presenter imparting information.
• Though often overlooked, setting an appropriate room temperature is essential for a comfortable meeting environment. Most people find the optimal room temperature to be between 68 and 72 degrees. Weather permitting, additional air circulation can be provided by opening doors and windows.
• Bright but indirect natural lighting is best; whenever possible, keep blinds open to take advantage of the sun. Low light makes work hard on the eyes and the nervous system, and can induce drowsiness.
• Excessive environmental noise can reduce comprehension and work performance. Be aware and attempt to reduce prominent sources of background noise in proximity to the workshop session.

The second important short-term preparation task is double-checking to make sure all materials are organized and working correctly. If using a computer slideshow, the presenter should do a dry run through all of the slides ensuring they can be seen by all participants. If that slideshow includes video clips, the presenter must make sure they work and that the volume can be raised loud enough to be heard by all.

Any teacher leader who leads enough presentations will eventually have something go wrong. When that happens, the teacher leader must improvise and demonstrate grace under pressure. However, the smart teacher leader seeks to avoid having anything go wrong that could have been prevented by advance preparation.

**Openings and Closings.** The opening and closing portion of any workshop are the two most important parts of any presentation. Therefore, these two times require additional considerations. As participants arrive, greet them if possible. The teacher leader should smile, introduce him or herself, and shake hands firmly. If it is a large group, circulate around the room and greet tables. Be clear, enthusiastic, and approachable. Participants' first impression will help them decide if the presenter is someone worth listening to.

Most likely, the teacher leader will introduce him or herself. When doing so, it is best to keep it brief, enthusiastic, and focused on the workshop content. A simple beginning to a self-introduction might be: "Good morning. I'm Matt Jennings and I am excited to be here to present *From First Year to First Rate*. I am looking forward to working with you to continue the great work you have been doing on mentoring. At the end of this session, you will have new ideas for how to include instructional coaching in your mentoring program."

The audience will remember best that which comes last. There are three goals for the closing section of a workshop. First, the teacher leader should strive to help the learners make connections among the sometimes-disparate segments of content included in the training. It is important to tie the pieces together into a unified whole. Second, participants must develop an action plan for how they are going to apply what they have learned to their own classroom. Third, the workshop needs to end on a high note. Participants need to feel positive about the experience.

**Oral Presentation Skills.** When a presenter shares information, the participants not only hear the content but also pay attention to the presenter's style. Workshop participants will be more receptive to the content if they perceive the teacher leader to be kind, considerate, flexible, positive, and enthusiastic. All of your actions must convey these qualities, including your oral speaking skills. When speaking, the teacher leader should consider the following guidelines:

- Use a softer or louder voice to indicate urgency, exasperation, or importance.
- Drawing certain words out more slowly than others can signal that what is being said is especially important.
- Judiciously placed pauses can focus the audience's attention and provide participants the opportunity to process the speaker's message.
- Enunciating clearly is critical. Among the most common mistakes in this regard are running words together and trailing off at the end of sentences.
- Words like "um," "ah," "okay," "ya know," and "like" are examples of fillers that can grate on listeners' nerves, so work diligently to eliminate them.
- Never use sexist, racist, profane, or vulgar language. It is unprofessional.

**Nonverbal Behaviors.** The four principal types of nonverbal behavior important for a presenter are eye contact, facial expression, body position, and hand gestures.

Whereas averting your eyes expresses disinterest and dislike, direct eye contact communicates interest and helps establish a rapport with participants. When presenting, teacher leaders should avoid looking at the ceiling or floor or over the head of the audience. Instead, the teacher leader should make a conscious effort to scan the whole room and establish eye contact with everyone. When responding to someone, the teacher leader should begin by looking that person in the eye and then making eye contact with the remainder of the audience.

If you want to put participants at ease, the most important thing to do is smile, as this indicates warmth and openness in communication. Speakers who smile when appropriate are perceived as more intelligent and credible than those who do not, but only when those smiles are perceived as genuine (Friend & Cook, 2007).

Good posture conveys poise and confidence. When speaking to all participants, the teacher leader should plant his or her feet on the ground and avoid shifting his or her weight back and forth. Walking among the audience members can be a good idea, but pacing back and forth in the same spot is distracting.

Certain types of hand gestures—keeping palms open when discussing an idea, for example—convey openness. However, the teacher leader must avoid fidgeting with objects or keeping their hands in their pockets. Displaying these nonverbal behaviors will help the teacher leader appear calm, composed, and confident. As a result, teacher leaders will convey warmth, authority, and sincerity to workshop participants.

**Using Visual Aids.** Well-designed visual aids, presented effectively, increase the teacher leader's credibility with the audience. In a previous section, strategies were presented for the effective design of common visual aids. In this section, strategies for incorporating the use of visual aids into the delivery of content are provided.

Flip Chart Presentation Guidelines:

- Use sticky tabs to locate specific information on prepared charts.
- Pencil small cues for yourself in the margins of the flip chart.
- Don't try to talk and write at the same time.
- Turn the page out of sight when the information is no longer pertinent.
- If you are planning on hanging charts, place strips of masking tape on the back of the easel in advance.

Computer Slideshow Guidelines:

- Orient participants to the slide show—for example, say "here are three research-based guidelines for teaching new vocabulary words."
- When speaking, address your audience rather than speaking toward the screen.
- Turn off the lights immediately in front of the screen but keep the rest of them on.

**Time Management.** As the leader of the workshop, the teacher leader must effectively manage the group's time. To be respectful of those that are punctual, the teacher leader should avoid waiting for stragglers and should not spend time summarizing for those that come late. Late participants can catch up on their own or can be brought up to speed on a break.

In addition, presenters must stick to the schedule. For example, if the workshop has time built in for lunch, then the teacher leader must pace the presentation in order to honor that time. Participants may have made advance plans for lunch.

Avoid allowing participants to ask questions that only relate to them. Taking time to answer questions that do not relate to the whole group will frustrate other participants. Instead, in the beginning of the presentation, request participants to record question unrelated to the needs or interests of the whole group on a sticky note and share it with you on a break or at another appropriate time.

The teacher leader facilitating a workshop must also contain digressions. Teacher leaders must not permit drawn-out personal examples or irrelevant tangents. Sometimes, it is necessary for the presenter to politely remind participants that statements must relate to the content and should be relevant to most in attendance.

When participants are working in groups, pay attention to the volume level of the voices. When the volume lowers, this means the groups are beginning to finish. This is the appropriate time to call "time" and review or go to the next point. Lastly, participants expect to end on time, and they always appreciate finishing a little bit early.

**Difficult Workshop Participants.** Some participants lack either the interpersonal skills or desire to work effectively in a large group setting. Others bring personal issues to the workshop setting that negatively influence their attitudes and actions. Regardless of the underlying reasons, these adults often display inappropriate behaviors which disrupt the learning environment. The following are five common types of difficult participants with some suggestions for how to deal with each of them.

Naysayers are those who reflexively disagree with the suggestions of others. The following are three suggestions for working more effectively with naysayers. First, you can ask the naysayer to offer alternatives. Second, you ask the group for opinions on the naysayer's comments. Third, you can ask the naysayer to articulate, "what would have to change for the proposed solution to work?"

Aggressors are those who express disagreement inappropriately. If the aggressor's comment is not directed at an individual, it is best to ignore it until a break, when you can speak to the individual privately. If the statement is made directly to you, remain professional and respectful. Acknowledge that there are different ways to think about any given topic and avoid becoming defensive or getting into an argument.

Dominators attempt to control discussions with redundant or unnecessarily long responses. These participants love to share "war stories," ask meaningless questions, or tell others what to do. The following suggestions will help neutralize the negative impact caused by dominators. First, the teacher leader can break eye contact with the dominator and call on someone else by name to provide a suggestion. Second, the teacher leader can use timed turns during group activities. Third, when the dominator pauses for breath, the teacher leader can take the opportunity to ask for someone else's opinion. Lastly, if a domineering participant is talking at the same time as the teacher leader, he or she can use proximity and pause. Then ask, "I'm sorry. Do you have a question?"

Attention seekers are participants with the need to be the focal point. To work more effectively with attention seekers, ask them to help with tasks. This uses their desire for attention to your advantage. Additionally, if the attention-seeking behavior is not disruptive, ignore it by turning your back to the individual. They will get the message that the attention they seek will not be provided in response to inappropriate behavior.

Lastly, there are avoiders. Avoiders are the individuals that either cannot or will not focus on the task at hand. When avoiders engage in side conversations or are preoccupied with other tasks, casually walk toward them while continuing to present. Stand near them until they cease doing what they are doing. Another necessity when dealing with avoiders is structuring interactions among group members so that tasks are divided equally. Traditional group work will allow avoiders to have a "free ride."

As a last resort, the teacher leader may need to ask a difficult workshop participant to leave. The best way to do this is to call for a break and speak with the disruptive person privately.

The content of this chapter has focused on principles of adult learning, understanding and managing colleagues' reactions to change, and preparing and presenting a workshop. In the next chapter, the reader will learn the knowledge and skills necessary for instructional leadership. More specifically, the reader will learn how to work with colleagues to analyze data, provide instructional coaching, and lead curriculum development and revision.

*Chapter 6*

# Instructional Leadership

Leadership of curricular and instructional areas with a direct impact on student achievement is a vital aspect of successful schools. Realistically school leaders must often devote significant amounts of time to managerial tasks. Despite their best efforts, school leaders are not able to be deeply involved with specific areas of teaching and learning. Teacher leaders can assist school leaders by sharing the instructional leadership role. More specifically, teacher leaders can provide nonevaluative instructional coaching, leadership of curriculum development, and assistance with organizing, interpreting, and using student achievement data.

## INSTRUCTIONAL COACHING

Teacher coaching is a powerful means of helping teachers turn knowledge into practice. However, in order for coaching to be successful, it is necessary to use a structured approach. Similar to the traditional teacher evaluation model, teacher coaching includes a pre-observation meeting, observation, and a post-observation meeting. However, the content and tone of these activities are different from the traditional practice of teacher observation and evaluation.

When coaching teachers, the purpose of the pre-observation meeting is to discuss the needs of the teacher and students as well as to agree on the specific data the teacher leader will gather during the lesson. The teacher must complete the pre-observation conference protocol (figure 6.1) in advance and bring it with them to the pre-observation meeting. During this pre-observation meeting, the teacher leader and the teacher being coached mutually agree upon the observation focus.

## PRE-OBSERVATION MEETING PROTOCOL

This section is to be completed by the mentee in advance of the pre-observation meeting:

- What is the objective for this lesson?

- What, specifically, do you want me to look for?

- Is there anything specific you want me to know about this class or lesson prior to the observation?

- When will the observation be and for how long will it take place?

- When and where will we meet after the observation to reflect upon the lesson?

At the scheduled time, the teacher leader observes the lesson, collecting the information on the agreed-upon instructional focus area. The generic coaching observation form (figure 6.2) provides a model of how data could be collected. After collecting the data, the teacher leader must analyze it and determine the most effective means of sharing it with the observed teacher.

The post-observation meeting is for the teacher leader and the observed teacher to collaboratively interpret the data and set an improvement goal. The post-observation meeting protocol (see below) provides structure for this process. Upon conclusion of the post-observation meeting, the observed teacher will have set an improvement goal that can serve as the basis for another coaching cycle.

## POST-OBSERVATION MEETING PROTOCOL

- Observed teacher describes how he or she thinks the lesson went.
- Based upon the focus area for the observation, discuss what the teacher leader observed.

Table 6.1   Coaching Observation Form

| COACHING OBSERVATION FORM ||
|---|---|
| **Teacher Name:** | **Observer Name:** |
| **Date:** | **Time:** |
| **Instructional Focus:** ||
| *Teacher Evidence* | *Student Evidence* |
|  |  |
| *Observation Notes* | *Ideas and Questions* |
|  |  |

- Collaborative reflection on the observations—what does the gathered data mean?
- Collaborative discussion of observation results for future practice. What can the observed teacher do differently to improve and how can he or she do it?
- Set a S.M.A.R.T improvement goal for a future coaching session.

When providing feedback to the observed teacher, teacher leaders must remain cognizant of the fact that many teachers feel threatened by a close examination of their practice (Danielson, 2006). Giving effective feedback takes skill and sensitivity. Teacher leaders must strive to provide observed teachers with feedback that includes the following characteristics:

- Descriptive—Describes the situation or behavior in observable terms.
- Specific—Is as specific as possible, avoiding terms like "always" and "never."
- Nonevaluative—Avoids words that are judgmental in nature.
- Timely—Is provided as close as possible to the observation.
- Behavioral—Sticks to specific behaviors that can be observed and repeated or changed; avoids inferences.
- Factual—Provides data whenever possible to substantiate conclusions.
- Honest—Truthful but tactful.

## Curriculum Development and Revision

A second area of instructional leadership commonly delegated to teacher leaders is curriculum development and revision. Depending upon the content area, available resources, and scope of the project, the process of curriculum development and revision may be completed by an individual or small group. Other times, the curriculum development and revision process may require the leadership of a large team. The process described in this section of the chapter will remain the same. However, if a large team is involved, then increased coordination of the process will be required.

How many times have teachers been told to create or revise a curriculum without any knowledge or training in a curriculum development process? Far too often, teachers are directed by administrators to complete this task with nothing more than formatting guidance and some types of content requirements for the final product. As a result, some of these guides look impressive, but in fact are impractical and overwhelming. Other guides are so incoherent they are useless. When developing curriculum guides to be used by teachers, the overarching goal is to keep them as simple and clear as possible.

The following proven process for developing curriculum guides must be tailored to meet the needs and resources of a specific school district. As described, this process is intended to be used with multiple teachers of the same subject across a defined grade span (e.g., K–2, 3–5, etc.). The process can be modified for use by individuals or small teams.

## Prioritizing Learning Standards

The first step in the process is prioritizing the state learning standards. To do this, a strand from the curriculum is chosen. The teacher leader introduces or reviews the criteria and process for identifying priority standards. Each standard is rated using the following criteria:

- Does the student have to know the content of this standard in order to succeed with important future learning?
- Does the content of this standard have value for future use?
- Does the content of this standard contain skills or concepts that are at the core of more than one discipline?

For each "yes" answer, the standard is awarded 1 point, up to a maximum of 3 points per standard. Each participant is to read and independently rate each standard.

Once each participant has completed his or her individual ratings, the next step is to reach initial consensus by grade level. The goal is to reach consensus on a reasonable, limited number of high-priority items that all students need to know and be able to do by the end of each grade and/or course. Importantly, it is what students need to know and not what teachers prefer to teach.

If the process is being completed by groups, then each group will use a piece of chart paper to record and share their work. The title of the chart shall contain the grade level and name of the standard. Underneath the title, the full text for each priority standard will be recorded.

Once completed, these charts shall be posted horizontally, progressing from the earliest to latest grade in the span. The individuals completing each chart will share their selections while the remainder of the group looks for gaps, overlaps, and omissions. In particular, those that teach the subject in the grade level above and below must have the opportunity to ask questions and offer suggestions. This process is repeated for all of the strands of the subject area.

At the conclusion of this stage in the process, the curriculum developers will have completed a draft of the priority standards for the subject area by grade level. This draft should be published for other teachers of that grade level or subject area to review and comment upon. Once the comment period is completed, any appropriate revisions should be made.

## Unpacking the Priority Standards

Frequently, standards lack clarity, specificity, and explicit identification of levels of rigor. Only by examining the wording of the standard can educators conclude what a standard requires in terms of student learning outcomes. Thus, the next step in the process is "unpacking" the standards.

Unpacking a standard is the process of analyzing the wording of the standard to determine exactly what students need to know (concepts) and be able to do (skills). Concepts are important nouns or noun phrases, and skills are verbs. To "unwrap," underline the nouns or noun phrases that represent teachable concepts and circle only those verbs that represent what students need to do. To identify vocabulary words for instruction, list the domain-specific words that are essential for understanding the priority standard. The outcome of this step will be a completed graphic organizer like the one below (figure 6.1). The results are the learning targets for the priority standard.

| PRIORITY STANDARD: <br> Know the common estimate of Pi (3.14, 22/7) and use these values to estimate and calculate the circumference and the area of circles. Use the formulas for the circumference and area of a circle. ||
|---|---|
| Students will understand.... <br> 1. The common estimate of Pi. | Students will be able to... <br> 1. Estimate the circumference and area of a circle. <br> 2. Calculate the circumference and area of a circle. <br> 3. Use formulas for circumference and area of a circle. |
| DOMAIN SPECIFIC VOCABULARY WORDS – Circumference, Area ||

Figure 6.1 Example of an Unpacked Standard.

## Grouping and Sequencing Standards and Targets

Having identified the priority standards and unwrapped them to identify the learning targets, the next step is to group and sequence them. Groups can be organized in three ways. First, the groups can be focused on a specific portion of a larger subject or discipline. Second, the groups can emphasize connections to other topics within the same or different discipline. Third, the groups can emphasize a skill or skills taught in a discipline.

If it makes sense instructionally, learning targets may be distributed across more than one grouping. Once grouped, the standards and targets must be sequenced into a logical order for instruction. Once again, this draft of grouped, sequenced learning targets should be published for others teachers of that grade level or subject area to review and comment upon.

## Units of Instruction and Pacing Calendars

The grouped and sequenced standards and targets are the content of units of instruction. Typically, instructional units last between two and eight weeks. Each unit of instruction should be named based on the purpose and dominant focus throughout the unit.

A pacing calendar is a year-long or course-long schedule for delivering all of the identified units of instruction for a designated grade level or course. The purpose of the pacing calendar is to ensure that all students learn all of the grade- or course-specific priority standards and their related learning targets in the correct order through a sequenced implementation of the units.

A pacing calendar should include a "Buffer Week" after each unit of instruction. The purpose of this interval between units of study is to provide time for remediation with students that do not demonstrate proficiency while providing proficient and advanced proficient students with time for appropriate enrichment activities.

To develop a pacing calendar, curriculum developers must first determine the approximate length of time required to implement the unit of instruction. Second, the units must be sequenced in the pacing calendar. When making this decision, curriculum developers should consider content that needs to be taught prior to standardized testing, as well as content that needs to be taught earlier in the year so that it can be reinforced throughout the year. The units of study and buffer weeks must fit within the total number of available instructional weeks. Figure 6.2 is part of a template that can be used to create a pacing calendar.

| PACING CALENDAR ||
|---|---|
| SUBJECT: | GRADE LEVEL: |
| QUARTER ONE ||
| NAME OF UNIT | TIME FRAME |
|  |  |
| BUFFER WEEK ||
|  |  |
| BUFFER WEEK ||
|  |  |
| BUFFER WEEK ||
| QUARTER TWO ||

**Figure 6.2   Partial Pacing Calendar Template.**

**Create the Big Ideas and Essential Questions.** Big ideas represent the foundational understandings (main ideas, conclusions, or generalizations) related to a unit's identified concepts. They are what educators want their students to discover and be able to state in their own words by the end of a unit of study. Big ideas represent the content educators want students to remember long after the instruction ends.

Big ideas can be broad, topical, or both. Broad big ideas are generalizations derived from one area of study that can be equally applicable to other areas of study. For example, "people interpret information and draw conclusions both from what they read and from what they experience" is a big idea that is important to a vast number of areas of study.

On the other hand, topical big ideas clearly relate to only one content area. The statement "mathematical formulas and estimations provide shortcuts for determining needed mathematical information" is only appropriate to mathematics. Occasionally, a big idea can be both broad and topical. The statement "objects can be compared and sorted by their attributes" is appropriate for both math and science.

Big ideas are the students' responses to essential questions. Essential questions begin with words like "how" and "why." For example, "why learn mathematical formulas?" and "how do estimation and formulas work together?" are both essential questions that lead to the big idea, "mathematical formulas and estimates both provide shortcuts for determining needed mathematical information." It is easier to write the essential questions after big ideas have been identified. One goal of instruction is for all students to be able to respond accurately in their own words to each of the units' essential questions.

**Proficiency Scales.** Using a taxonomy like Bloom's, the learning targets for each priority standard are sequenced in the order of complexity from low to high. Rank-ordered learning targets become the content of priority standard proficiency scales. The starting point for the proficiency scale of a prioritized learning standard is level 3.0. This is the target learning goal for all of the students.

Level 4.0 learning goals are more complex. The expectation for these learning targets is that some, if any, students will achieve this level of learning. Level 2.0 is for the simpler learning goals. Level 2.0 is the most basic content required for achieving proficiency toward the learning standard. Figure 6.3 is a proficiency scale for the unwrapped priority learning standard shared earlier in the chapter

**Common Assessments.** Proficiency scales become the basis for creating common pre- and post-assessments for each unit of study. The format of the assessments should be questions addressing level 2.0 expectations for a

| PRIORITY STANDARD: | |
|---|---|
| Know the common estimate of Pi (3.14, 22/7) and use these values to estimate and calculate the circumference and the area of circles. Use the formulas for the circumference and area of a circle. | |
| Students will understand…. <br> 1. The common estimate of Pi. | Students will be able to… <br> 1. Estimate the circumference and area of a circle. <br> 2. Calculate the circumference and area of a circle. <br> 3. Use formulas for circumference and area of a circle. |
| DOMAIN SPECIFIC VOCABULARY WORDS – Circumference, Area | |
| Level 4.0 | **Students will be able to:** <br> * Use knowledge of Pi and the formulas for circumference and area of a circle to determine how far a car has traveled based on the radius of a tire. |
| Level 3.5 | In addition to score 3.0 performance, partial success at 4.0 content. |
| Level 3.0 | **Students will be able to:** <br> * Estimate the circumference and area of a circle. <br> * Calculate the circumference and area of a circle. |
| Level 2.5 | No major errors or omissions regarding score 2.0 content, and partial success at score 3.0 content. |
| Level 2.0 | **Students will understand:** <br> * The common estimate of Pi. <br> * The terms circumference and area. |
| Level 1.5 | Partial success at score 2.0 content. |
| Level 1.0 | No success at score 2.0 content. |

**Figure 6.3   Example Proficiency Scale.**

standard, followed by level 3.0 questions for that same standard. This makes it possible to use the previously developed proficiency scales to evaluate student performance. Common assessments should be published for other teachers of that subject area and/or grade level to review and comment on before being finalized.

**Unit Design Template**. The following template (figure 6.4) is an example of how the content of each unit can be organized. For the listed learning targets, a suggested timeframe for the number of instructional periods for that target is to be included. In addition, formative assessment opportunities should be inserted at the points where it would make sense for the teacher to conduct a whole-class assessment of student progress. Completed unit templates should be shared with teachers of that subject area and/or grade level prior to being finalized.

Having followed this curriculum development process, the result will be a common pacing chart that identifies the units of instruction for the year. For each identified unit of instruction, teachers will have a common unit outline that contains the essential questions, big ideas, prioritized learning standards,

| Unit Title: | |
|---|---|
| Grade Level: | |
| Timeframe: | |
| **Essential Question(s)** | |
| | |
| **Big Idea(s)** | |
| | |
| **Sequenced Prioritized Standards** | |
| | |
| **Instructional Plan** | |
| Pre-Assessment: | |
| **Learning Target** | **Suggested Pacing** |
| | |
| | |
| | |
| Formative Assessment: | |
| | |
| | |
| | |
| Formative Assessment: | |
| | |
| | |
| Summative Assessment: | |

**Figure 6.4  Unit Template.**

and an instructional plan. The instructional plan will include a common pre- and post-unit assessment. These assessments will provide data to be used to make informed instructional decisions. Collecting, organizing, analyzing, and using student data is the subject of the next section of this chapter.

**Data Use.** Assessment results must be more than sources of data for grades or records in cumulative files. Instead, assessment results must serve as discussion opportunities that ultimately lead to improved instruction and student achievement. A growing body of research evidence suggests that when teachers collaborate to pose and answer questions about data collected from their own students, their knowledge grows and their practices change (David, 2009). However, these instructional improvements will not occur if the process for analyzing the data is flawed.

**Quality Data.** Teachers cannot draw accurate inferences about student learning from invalid assessments. In other words, student achievement data is only as good as the quality of the assessment tools used to collect that data. Effective data-driven instruction is impossible unless schools invest in creating or acquiring valid assessments. Teacher leaders must be aware of the quality of the assessment tool used when working with teachers to draw conclusions about students and make instructional decisions. Not all data is worth using; this is a profound, but too often overlooked, truth (Popham, 2009).

Another issue with regard to data quality is timing. If teachers do not view the assessment data as timely, then efforts to get them to use that data fall flat (David, 2009). Furthermore, every day that passes between the administration of the assessment and the analysis of the results is another day in which new material is taught without correcting errors and misconceptions. The best data for instructional decision-making comes from assessments that have been recently administered.

A major challenge in education is not the lack of available data, but drowning in too much of it (Bambrick-Santoyo, 2019). Effective use of data requires sharpening the focus so it is manageable for teachers. The more complicated and voluminous the data-collection process and corresponding information, the less likely the teachers are to use it.

In sum, the best data processes use valid tools to collect only the most meaningful student data. Furthermore, collected data is shared through a simple format in a timely manner. These two statements are true regardless of whether the data is collected for the whole school, by grade or subject level, or by individuals.

**Standardized Tests.** Teacher leaders may be part of whole-school data conversations. The source for whole-school data conversations is commonly standardized tests. Even though standardized assessments may be valid, they are neither timely nor are they user-friendly. Yet, schools spend inordinate amounts of time on setting achievement goals and measuring progress toward these goals for standardized testing. Until this situation changes, teacher leaders must know how to interpret the data from these tests if they are to meaningfully contribute to the discussion.

Standardized tests are either norm-referenced or criterion-referenced. Norm-referenced tests are used to compare how a test-taker performs relative to other test-takers. To create this comparison, test data are converted to the normal curve so that scores can be compared to a larger population of test-takers. In principle, the sample size of the test-takers is large enough, and the sampling procedures are accurate enough, that results approximate the general population—and therefore fall into a normal (bell-shaped) curve. Any subsample taken from the larger pool of data can be understood and compared using standard scores and positions. To interpret the results of norm-referenced tests requires understanding of the following specific measurement terms:

- Raw score—a numerical count of the number of items the student answered correctly, or the sum of all the points awarded to the student's responses.
- Standard score—a raw score that has been redefined in terms of a standard, constant mean and a standard, constant standard deviation.
- Percent correct score—number correct divided by the total number of items.
- Norm group—the group of students used to set the score scales.
- Percentile rank—a description of a student's score relative to other test-takers. The percentile rank describes where the student scored in comparison to the norm group. Percentile ranks range from 1 to 99. By definition, the score tells what percentage of the norm group the student scored better than.
- Stanine—a scale with nine points. Stanines slice the normal curve into nine categories with a mean of 5 and a standard deviation of 1.96. Three of the points (7, 8, 9) describe performance above the average and three of the points (1, 2, 3) describe performance below the average. Stanine scores are derived from percentile scores.
- Quartiles—numbers that divide ranked data into quarters. Each set of data has three quartiles. The upper limit of the first quartile is the number at which ¼ of all of the scores fall below that value. At the upper limit of the second quartile, half of the data points fall below that number. The third quartile is the number for which ¾ of the population earned a lower score.

Criterion-referenced tests are designed to identify what a test-taker knows in relation to specific objectives. Standards-based, criterion-referenced assessments allow schools to compare how students perform against a predetermined, specified standard of performance. Cut scores are the score on criterion-referenced tests that determine the test-taker's level of proficiency. Example terms used to describe performance levels include advanced proficient, proficient, and partially proficient.

Potentially far more meaningful to the improvement of instruction is the use of teacher-created assessments. Teachers trained in research-based methods of creating assessments can produce interim assessments precisely matching the curriculum scope and sequence. In this situation, the degree of alignment between what the teacher is teaching and the content of the assessment should be high. In addition, the results from teacher-created assessments can be ascertained quickly.

Yet, if these test results are to have a significant impact, they must be used for more than providing grades to students. Instead, they should serve as a means for teachers to fine-tune instruction in a manner that enables all students to be successful (Neuman, 2016). The organization, analysis, and use of data is an area for which the assistance of knowledgeable teacher leaders can be extremely valuable.

**Data Analysis**. Teachers are more likely to collect and use data systematically when working as a group. When working by themselves, teachers tend to rely on anecdotes and intuition (David, 2009). Thus, whenever possible, teacher leaders should strive to work with groups of teachers sharing common assessment data.

Teacher groups have more productive data discussions when they work from an approachable data set that has been carefully prepared to spotlight patterns and trends in student learning. A class profile graph, item analysis graph, and non-mastery report are three formats that can be used primarily for making instructional decisions.

Tables of item difficulty and item discrimination are useful for scrutinizing the quality of test items. Generating these two types of reports takes time and effort. Thus, they should only be created and used for assessments that require detailed analysis. An example of a type of assessment worthy of this time and effort are the common unit assessments described in the previous section on curriculum development.

**Data for Instructional Decision-Making**. The class profile graph plots every student in the class that took the assessment and how they scored overall. Through gathering this information, the teacher can determine which students are reaching the desired level of proficiency. This graph requires that every student in the class is listed along the Y-axis, and his or her percentage score is plotted on the X-axis. Figure 6.5 is an example class profile graph.

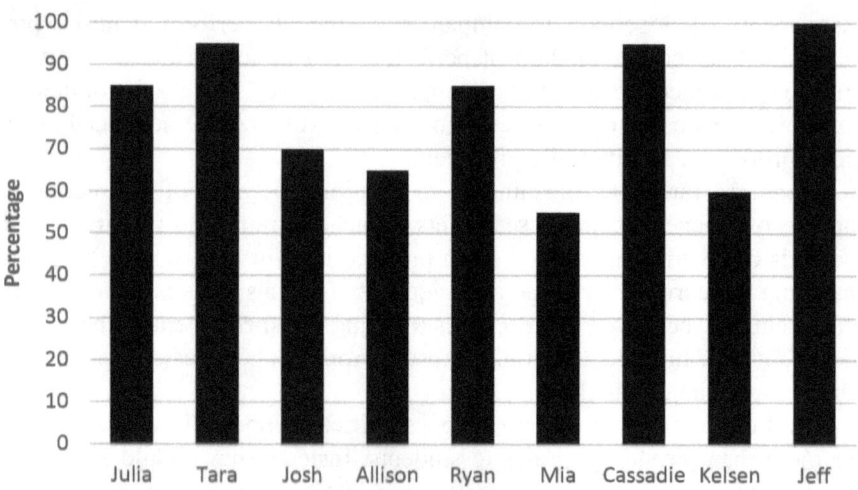

**Figure 6.5  Class Profile Graph.**

The essence of successful discussion about data is a commitment to examine not only the data but also the stories behind the numbers (Reeves, 2009). When examining the data illustrated by a class profile graph, the following questions can be used for analysis:

- How did the class perform as a whole?
- Do the results of individual students make sense?
- If the results attained by an individual student do not make sense, why might this be the case?

An item analysis graph is a chart that displays the average of how the class performed on each question. The Y-axis represents each question identified by number and standard. The X-axis represents the percentage of students that demonstrate proficiency for that question. Figure 6.6 is an example of an Item Analysis Graph.

When examining the data illustrated by an item analysis graph, the following questions can be used to guide the analysis of the data:

- What are the strengths and weaknesses in the standards? Where did the students perform best and worst?
- Within one standard, did students do similarly on every question, or were some questions harder? If so, why?
- Did the results differ based on question type? Did students score better or worse on constructed response versus selected response items?

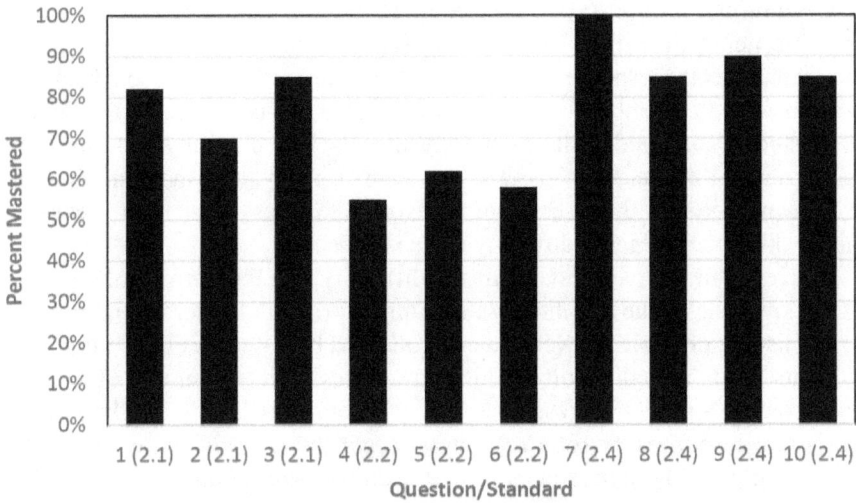

**Figure 6.6 Item Analysis Graph.**

A non-mastery report is a combination of the class profile graph and classroom item analysis graph. To develop a non-mastery report, list each question, standard number, and the students that did not answer it correctly. This list will give the teacher an indication of how they might group students for reteaching. If the number of students for a specific question is large, then the teacher may need to reteach that standard to the entire class. Table 6.2 is an example of a blank template that can be used to generate a non-mastery report.

**Table 6.2  Non-Mastery Report**

| | |
|---|---|
| Question # | Standard # |
| Students recording incorrect responses: | |
| | |
| Question # | Standard # |
| Students recording incorrect responses: | |
| | |
| Question # | Standard # |
| Students recording incorrect responses: | |

## Chapter 6

**Evaluating the Quality of an Assessment.** If the assessment contains selected response items, then those items can be further analyzed. The difficulty of an individual selected response item is calculated by dividing the number of students who answered correctly by the number of total students answering the item. If every student answered the item correctly, then the item difficulty score would be 1.0. If none of the students answered the item correctly, then the item difficulty score would be 0. If the assessment is designed to assess mastery of previously taught skills, then a higher difficulty score is expected.

To create an item analysis chart for difficulty, list the item numbers vertically down the farthest right-hand column. Horizontally, across the top columns, list the possible answer choices, followed by columns titled "number of students" and "item difficulty." Fill in the boxes with the number of students that selected a particular response for each item. Finally, divide the number of correct responses by total responses to get the item difficulty. Table 6.3 is an example of an item analysis chart used for determining item difficulty.

**Table 6.3  Item Difficulty Chart**

| Item Number | A | B | C | D | Number of Students | Item Difficulty |
|---|---|---|---|---|---|---|
| 1 | 0 | **10** | 0 | 0 | 10 | 1.0 |
| 2 | **8** | 1 | 1 | 0 | 10 | 0.8 |
| 3 | 2 | **8** | 0 | 0 | 10 | 0.8 |
| 4 | 6 | 1 | **3** | 0 | 10 | 0.3 |
| 5 | 3 | 2 | 0 | **5** | 10 | 0.5 |
| 6 | 2 | 3 | 3 | **2** | 10 | 0.2 |
| 7 | **5** | 1 | 1 | 3 | 10 | 0.5 |

- Numbers in bold indicate the number of students that selected the correct response.

Examination of the data contained in an item difficulty chart can then be guided by the following questions:

- Are there patterns in the number of students who chose a wrong answer?
- Did the majority of students choose the same wrong answer on a question? If so, why?

Examination of the aforementioned data set provides observations requiring further investigation. For example, only three students chose the correct answer on item 4. Interestingly, six of the seven students who chose the wrong answer selected A as the correct response. What was it about that answer choice that caused so many students to pick it incorrectly? Item 6 had only two students choose the correct answer. However, in this case, selection of the incorrect choice was distributed more evenly. This suggests that all of the answer choices were plausible.

Another analysis of question results can be achieved through examining item discrimination. Item discrimination is an indication of how effective a test item is at distinguishing between students who know the material tested and those who do not. To create a table for analyzing item discrimination, students are listed in the order of their test scores from highest to lowest. Along the top of the table, the item numbers are listed. The body of the table indicates whether the student answered correctly (*) and, if not, which incorrect response was chosen. Table 6.4 is an example of an item discrimination table.

**Table 6.4  Item Discrimination Table**

| Students | #1 | #2 | #3 | #4 | #5 | #6 | #7 |
|---|---|---|---|---|---|---|---|
| Tara | * | * | * | * | * | * | * |
| Cassadie | * | * | A | * | * | * | B |
| Josh | * | * | A | * | * | * | B |
| Ryan | * | * | A | * | * | * | B |
| Allison | * | A | * | * | A | C | C |
| Mia | * | B | C | * | B | C | D |
| Kelsen | * | C | B | * | D | C | C |

If you draw an imaginary line across the middle of this table (Ryan), you divide the class into the top half of scorers and the bottom half of scorers. In looking at the mistakes made, it becomes obvious that questions 3 and 7 presented problems for the higher scorers. In addition, the higher scores chose the same incorrect response.

This pattern represents potentially valuable information. More specifically, because these students demonstrated otherwise correct knowledge, these two items require further examination to determine if there is an element of truth in the incorrect response. Perhaps if these students were asked to explain the rationale for their selection, they may share the same misunderstanding of what the item asked for.

In addition, note that only high scorers selected the correct response for items 2 and 5. This suggests that these two items are effective at discriminating between those who know the content of the assessment and those that do not. Lastly, for item 6, all those who answered the item incorrectly were low scorers who selected the same response. The fact that they held the same misconception may suggest a clear instructional intervention for these students.

Regardless of the content of the data analysis process, one thing must remain constant. Participating teachers must believe that the data will not be used as punishment. Instead, teacher leaders must reassure colleagues that examination of results with the aim of improving student learning does not suggest criticism. Rather, data analysis represents a joint effort by colleagues to achieve better results for students.

This chapter has prepared the teacher leader to share the responsibilities of instructional leadership. More specifically, this chapter provided teacher leaders with knowledge and skills related to instructional coaching, curriculum development, and data analysis. The focus of the final chapter is the teacher leader's role in human resource management.

*Chapter 7*

# Human Resources Management

It is a generally accepted fact that high-quality instruction is positively related to increased student achievement. Conversely, low-quality instruction can have negative impacts with long-lasting repercussions for students. In short, if schools are to succeed in their mission to promote high levels of student achievement, the quality of teaching matters.

Of course, it is necessary to have quality teachers in order to provide quality teaching. Nothing is more important to student achievement than recruiting, hiring, developing, and retaining excellent staff. Yet, annually, school administrators attempt to complete the recruiting and hiring process without the help of the experts in their own buildings.

How a teacher is hired is likely to affect his or her job satisfaction and retention (Clement, 2013). Involving teacher leaders in the recruiting and hiring process provides job candidates with realistic information about students, curriculum, and the workplace. This information will help candidates better judge if the position is a potentially good fit.

Furthermore, even though the school leader may have sufficient knowledge of effective instructional practices, they are unlikely to have expertise in the application of that knowledge to various subjects and grade levels. Through participation in the interview process, teacher leaders are able to ascertain the depth of a candidate's subject-matter knowledge in a way that most school leaders can't.

Thus, a potentially important role for teacher leaders is participation in the recruitment and hiring of staff. Additionally, once new staff are hired, teacher leaders can play an important role in their induction and mentoring.

**Recruitment.** One potential pool of applicants is substitute and student teachers. Often, as a result of their experiences long-term substitutes and student teachers have completed "an extended job interview." The quality of their work can be observed in a close approximation of the context in which they would be employed. Also, the quality of their interactions with current staff can be ascertained. It is much more likely that a good approximation of the fit between the candidate, the position, and the school can be determined by student and long-term substitute teaching than through the typical interview process.

However, an employer's determination of the fit between the candidate, position, and school is only half of the process. Through their experience serving as a student or long-term substitute teacher, the candidate must want to work in that school or district. Teacher leaders can assume responsibility for making sure student teachers and long-term substitutes have positive and productive experiences.

Even if the long-term substitute or student teacher is not a potential hire, it is very likely they have friends and colleagues. The quality of the experience they had while working in a school will be shared with these friends and colleagues. These shared experiences impact a school's reputation. A positive reputation goes a long way toward increasing the quality and quantity of candidate pools for new hires.

Another source of recruitment for future teachers is job fairs. Typically, these job fairs are attended by human resource representatives from a school district. It is a mistake to exclude teacher leaders from this process. Potential candidates will have questions only an experienced teacher can answer. In addition, involving teacher leaders as representatives at job fairs makes a strong statement regarding the value a school or district places on their instructional staff.

**Interviewing**. From the outset, the roles and responsibilities for teacher leaders within the interview process must be made clear. This is especially true for how final decisions regarding candidates will be made. If the school leader has the final say over who gets hired, that should be communicated upfront. Clarity regarding decision-making roles avoids misunderstandings and hard feelings.

The most common role for a teacher leader in the interview process is as a member of a selection committee. This role requires the teacher leader to accurately judge the quality of candidate's responses and then articulate reasons for those judgments to other committee members. Thus, if teacher leaders are to effectively fill the role of a staff-selection committee member, they must develop the skills required to make sound judgments of candidates.

During the interview, candidates can use a variety of tactics to manage interviewers' impressions. These include excessive self-promotion and ingratiation by telling the interviewers' what they think they want to hear. By exaggerating their qualities, inventing experiences, and omitting information, candidates can obtain higher ratings. The goal of the interviewers is to hire a candidate who actually has the right profile for the job, not the one who can best pretend to be a good fit.

In general, relying on interviewers to identify and eliminate fakers is doomed to lead to failure. Research demonstrates that interviewers are largely incapable of accurately detecting influence tactics (Roulin, 2017). This is largely due to interviewers' reliance on the wrong cues to detect deception.

Focusing on invalid nonverbal behaviors, such as gaze avoidance, instead of valid verbal information will usually result in bad decisions. The focus must be on responses that give fewer details about experiences and stories that are more impersonal, more evasive, and less logically structured.

Furthermore, interviewers must be aware of unconscious cognitive biases when judging applicants. The assessment of candidates can be influenced by factors such as initial impressions, similarity effects, halo effects, and contrast effects. These biases are likely to impair the interviewers' ability to effectively assess the true qualifications of a candidate.

Interviewers usually form an initial impression of an applicant within the first few minutes of the interview. Once this impression is formed, interviewers tend to engage in the process of confirming their initial impressions. In other words, during the remainder of the interview, the interviewer sets up the candidates to respond in a way that confirms their initial impression, and then interprets the candidate's responses as proof that their initial impression was correct. Oftentimes, these initial impressions are based on irrelevant information. Interviewers must be aware of this risk.

We tend to like people who demonstrate qualities similar to ourselves. Thus, an applicant who appears similar to us may be viewed as a good fit for the position. We also tend to favor candidates who share our demographic characteristics. Teacher leaders must use awareness of this potential bias to decrease the impact of these similar-to-me effects.

Another potential bias is the halo effect. It is a natural tendency to rely on beliefs that some traits or characteristics are automatically associated, that is, if a person has trait A, then they must also have trait B. A common example of this is the association of those that are physically attractive with more positive personality characteristics. This can work in both a positive (halo) and negative (horn) manner. To avoid making these associations, interviewers must be aware of their existence and avoid extrapolating information based on unrelated characteristics.

Lastly, as a series of interviews progresses, we may demonstrate bias when comparing applicants to one another. In other words, the assessment of one applicant can be influenced by the assessment of previous candidates. The same candidate with average qualifications can be rated more positively if he or she follows a series of poorly qualified candidates. The opposite is also true.

Teacher leaders who can make sound judgments regarding potential candidates will improve the hiring process. They will add perspective likely to be missing if the process only involves school leaders. In addition to their role in recruiting and interviewing, teacher leaders should play a significant role in the induction and mentoring of new hires.

**Mentoring and Induction.** Employment as a new staff member in a school district commonly begins with an orientation program. When preparing an orientation program, teacher leaders must provide an opportunity for new staff to clarify job responsibilities and expectations, learn about the history of the school district, meet fellow teachers and staff members, understand policies and procedures, and become comfortable with the new work environment (Tomal et al., 2014). After the orientation, subsequent activities for new hires should be differentiated.

It is important to distinguish between new hires who are also new teachers and new hires that are experienced teachers. The needs of these two groups are different. Teacher leaders should work with school leaders to create definitions for these two groups and then provide different and appropriate types of support (Carr et al., 2005). New hires that are new teachers also benefit from a well-designed, formal mentoring program.

For mentoring to be successful, it must be one part of a larger, structured induction process. According to Smith & Ingersoll (2004), the support of a mentor alone is a practice that only reduces five-year teacher attrition rates by one percentage point. Yet, as one part of an overall induction program, mentoring can help novice teachers face the challenges of teaching. Mentors can engage mentees through reflective activities and professional conversations as well as provide social-emotional support.

Additionally, mentoring can foster the professional development of mentors. Mentoring encourages veteran teachers to improve themselves, receive respect, develop collegiality, and profit from novice teachers' fresh ideas and energy. Done properly, mentoring has benefits for both the mentor and the mentee (Breaux, 2016).

To be clear, there is nothing beneficial about a haphazard mentoring process. If it is to be effective, a mentoring program must be focused and structured. Mentoring programs require thoughtful planning and quality professional development to ensure that the relationship between mentor and mentee is productive (Carr et al., 2005). More specifically, there must be a systematic selection process, clarity regarding roles and responsibilities, adequate training to meet those responsibilities, and time for collaboration.

**Mentor Selection.** Unfortunately, mentors are often chosen for the wrong reasons. It may be that they are the only willing volunteers or those that seek financial compensation for performing the role. Perhaps little thought is given to the selection of the mentor. Yet, having no mentor is better than having an ineffective one.

Teachers chosen as mentors must be respected by colleagues for their knowledge and expertise as teachers, have a strong interest in learning, and have a history of working respectfully and supportively with colleagues. If we want new teachers to be effective and to stay in teaching, then only our most effective teachers should be selected for the mentoring role.

In addition, a person with an attitude that falls short of true professionalism should never serve as a mentor for a new teacher. Even if they are a good teacher within the walls of their own classroom, the damage they do to a new teacher's attitude toward teaching can be long lasting and pervasive. Regardless of the process used to select mentors, the goal should be to select the best, and only the best, for this role. Teacher leaders can assist school leaders with the selection and pairing of mentors and mentees.

**Mentor Roles and Responsibilities**. Mentors must have a clear understanding of their roles and responsibilities. A mentor teacher is one that serves as a role model. Through their example, they demonstrate how to handle difficult conversations and sensitive situations.

Mentors serve as informal guides on how things work within a school and a district. They guide novice teachers in completing the multitude of procedures required in the regular operation of schools. They also help novice teachers understand the unwritten norms for behavior that exist within a school.

Novice teachers require emotional support. The first years of teaching are stressful and can be overwhelming. Through a trusting relationship characterized by active listening and encouragement, mentor teachers can provide this support. The importance of the relationship between a mentor and a mentee cannot be stressed enough. A new teacher has to trust a mentor enough to share both successes and mistakes.

One of the more overwhelming aspects of being a novice teacher is the lack of guidance and resources they receive for instructional planning. 41 percent of first-year teachers surveyed nationwide stated that their schools or districts provide them with few or no instructional resources (Matthews, 2011).

Although such curricular freedom may be cherished by veteran teachers, it is a burden for new teachers. Novice teachers have yet to develop a robust repertoire of lesson ideas and instructional materials. A mentor can provide these resources through sharing instructional plans and proven classroom materials. Of course, this is much easier to do if the mentor and mentee share the same content area and/or grade level for instruction. Teacher leaders can help mentors understand and fulfill their roles as informal guides, emotional supports, and sources of guidance for instructional planning.

**Mentor Training and Support**. An effective mentoring program requires providing mentors with professional development designed to address the content, timing, and communication of mentoring support (Carr et al., 2005). One aspect of this training should be facilitating mentors' understanding that the nature of support required changes based on the time of the school year.

New teachers go through predictable stages during their first year in the classroom. Each stage is associated with emotions and challenges. The month of August is the anticipation phase. As new teachers strive to get organized for the year and learn basic procedures and policies of the school, they experience a combination of excitement and anxiety.

The first month of school is very overwhelming for new teachers. They are expected to learn a lot of new information at a very rapid pace. New teachers are frequently caught off-guard by the realities of teaching. During this survival phase, new teachers struggle to keep their heads above water and become very focused and consumed with the day-to-day routine of teaching. There is little time to stop and reflect on their experiences as they are likely spending up to seventy hours a week on school-related work.

After six to eight weeks of nonstop work and stress, new teachers enter a phase characterized by disillusionment. The extensive time commitment and the realization that things are not going as planned despite these efforts results in a period of disenchantment. During this time, new teachers question their commitment and their competence. Getting through this phase is likely to be the toughest challenge faced as a new teacher.

Generally beginning in January, a period of rejuvenation begins. This phase is characterized by a slow improvement in the new teacher's attitude toward teaching. Coming off winter break, novice teachers emerge with a broader perspective and a renewed sense of hope—a better understanding of the system, an acceptance of the realities of teaching, and a sense of accomplishment help to rejuvenate new teachers.

Starting in May, new teachers enter the reflection phase. As they reflect back over the events of the year, they make a note of things that were successful and those that weren't. This information is used to think about the various changes they intend to make in management, curriculum, and instruction for the subsequent school year. This emerging vision for the future brings them to a new phase of anticipation.

Teacher leaders can create and provide a structured calendar of activities for mentors to use to successfully support mentees. These activities should be aligned to the needs associated with the previously identified stages. In addition, they must coordinate with the expectations of the school and district. Table 7.1 is an example of a partially completed calendar for mentors.

Table 7.1  Sample Mentoring Calendar

| October Mentoring Calendar | | |
|---|---|---|
| Informational Tasks | Instructional Tasks | Management Tasks |
| • Debrief department, grade level, team, and/or committee meeting.<br>• Help prepare for parent-teacher conferences.<br>• Jointly review progress reports. | • Jointly review content and format of lesson plans.<br>• Discuss how classroom management plans are going.<br>• Encourage saving student work samples for parent-teacher conferences. | • Discuss how to set up parent-teacher conferences.<br>• Discuss how to enter final grades for the quarter.<br>• Review how to apply to attend a conference. |

Novice teachers yearn for, but seldom receive, meaningful feedback on their instructional practices from veteran colleagues (McCormack et al., 2006). Regrettably, Fry (2007) found that mentor teachers assigned to provide this support were sometimes part of the problem. He concluded that mentors dispensed little guidance, if not bad advice.

Properly trained mentors can provide coaching through the modeling of effective strategies and objective observations of mentees' instruction. Knowing how to teach and knowing how to teach someone else to teach are two very different skill sets. To be effective, mentors need knowledge of how to support new teachers and the skill at providing guidance. In addition, mentor teachers need support and the opportunity to discuss ideas, problems, and solutions with other mentor teachers. Teacher leaders can facilitate mentor sharing sessions.

**Collaboration Time**. Finally, mentor teachers need time to both observe and reflect upon instruction with their mentees. Perhaps they have reduced teaching loads or substitute coverage is provided in order to complete their mentoring responsibilities. If necessary, teacher leaders can provide this coverage or assist with scheduling substitute teachers.

It is counterproductive to make serving as a mentor an overwhelming task. Without time, mentors and mentees will become frustrated, making it very difficult to build the types of supportive relationships that benefit both the mentor and the new teacher. This mentoring relationship is too precious to risk allowing to fail because of a lack of time for collaboration.

This chapter has addressed the role of the teacher leader in human resources management. Teacher leaders can play an important role in the recruitment, selection, and support of new hires. Fulfilling assigned and appropriate responsibilities in the area of human resources is yet another way teacher leaders can improve the quality of teaching in a school.

With clearly defined responsibilities and conducive conditions, the right teachers can lead colleagues toward improvement of their school's instructional program. However, achieving high-impact teacher leadership requires time, effort, and resources. Those involved with promoting teacher leadership must have the fortitude required to take the actions described in this book. Through these actions, teacher leaders will directly impact the growth and development of colleagues, which in turn will lead to increased student achievement. This desired state of affairs describes a better future for our students and the adults that work every day to serve them.

# Bibliography

Bambrick-Santoyo, P. (2019). *Driven by data 2.0: A practical guide to improve instruction.* San Francisco, CA: Jossey Bass.
Barth, R.S. (2002). The culture builder. *Educational Leadership,* 59 (8), 6–11.
Barth, R.S. (2013). The time is ripe again. *Educational Leadership,* 71 (2), 10–16.
Beachum, F. & Dentith, A.M. (2004). Teacher leaders creating cultures of school renewal and transformation. *The Educational Forum,* 68 (3).
Brandon, R. & Seldman, M. (2004). *Survival of the savvy: High integrity political tactics for career and company success.* New York, NY: Free Press.
Breaux, A. (2016). Ten ways to make mentoring work. *Educational Leadership,* 73 (8).
Carr, J.F., Herman, N. & Harris, D.E. (2005). *Creating dynamic schools through mentoring, coaching and collaboration.* Alexandria, VA: Association for Supervision and Curriculum Development.
Carver-Thomas, D. & Darling-Hammond, L. (2017). *Teacher turnover: Why it matters and what we can do about it.* Palo Alto, CA: Learning Policy Institute.
Clement, M.C. (2013). Teachers hiring teaches. *Educational Leadership,* 71 (2).
Cloke, K. & Goldsmith, J. (2011). *Resolving conflicts at work: Ten strategies for everyone on the job* (3rd edition). San Francisco, CA: Jossey Bass.
Conyers, M. & Wilson, D. (2016). *Smarter teacher leadership: Neuroscience and the power of purposeful teacher collaboration.* New York, NY: Teachers College Press.
Danielson, C. (2006). *Teacher leadership that strengthens professional practice.* Alexandria, VA: Association for Supervision and Curriculum Development.
David, J.L. (2008). What research says about collaborative inquiry. *Educational Leadership,* 66 (4), 87–88.
Deal, T.E. & Peterson, K.D. (1999). *Shaping school culture: The heart of leadership.* San Francisco, CA: Jossey-Bass
Deluca, J.R. (1999). *Political savvy: Systematic approaches to leadership behind-the-scenes.* Berwyn, PA: EBG Publications.

Friend, M. & Cook, L. (2007). *Interactions: Collaboration skills for school professionals*. Boston, MA: Pearson Education.

Fry, S.W. (2007). *How it's being done: Urgent lessons from unexpected schools*. Cambridge, MA: Harvard Education Press.

Fullan, M. (2007). *The new meaning of educational change* (4th edition). New York, NY: Teachers College Press.

Gabriel, J.G. (2005). *How to thrive as a teacher leader*. Alexandria, VA: Association for Supervision and Curriculum Development.

Goddard, R., Goddard, Y., Kim, E.S. & Miller, R. (2015). A theoretical and empirical analysis of the roles of instructional leadership, teacher collaboration and collective efficacy beliefs in support of student learning. *American Journal of Education*, 121 (4).

Granger, R.H. (2008). *The 7 triggers to yes: The new science behind influencing people's decisions*. New York, NY: McGraw Hill.

Grissom, J.A., Loeb, S. & Master, B. (2013). Effective instructional time use for school leaders: Longitudal evidence from observation of principals. *Educational Researcher*, 42 (8).

Harris, T.E. (2002). *Applied organizational communication: Principles and pragmatics for future practices*. Mahwah, NJ: Lawrence Erlbaum Associates.

Hoerng, E. & Loeb, S. (2010). New thinking about instructional leadership, *Phi Delta Kappan*, 92 (3).

Ingersoll, R.M., Sirinides, P. & Dougherty, P. (2017). *School leadership, teachers' role in decision-making and student achievement*. Philadelphia, PA: Consortium for Policy Research in Education.

Katzenmyer, M. & Moller, G. (2009). *Awakening the sleeping giant: Helping teachers develop as leaders* (3rd edition). Thousand Oaks, CA: Corwin Press.

Levi, D. (2007). *Group dynamics for teams* (2nd edition). Thousand Oaks, CA: Sage Publications.

Levin, B.B. & Schrum, L. (2017). *Every teacher a leader: Developing the needed dispositions, knowledge and skills for teacher leadership*. Thousand Oaks, CA: Corwin Press.

Margolis, J. (2009). How teachers lead teachers. *Educational Leadership*, 66 (5).

Matthews, J. (2011, December 18). *New teacher decries lesson plan gap* (blog post). Retrieved from Class Struggle at the Washington Post.

McIntyre, M.G. (2005). *Secrets to winning at office politics: How to achieve your goals and increase your influence at work*. New York, NY: St. Martin's Press.

McCormack, A., Gore, J. & Thomas, K. (2006). Early career teacher professional learning. *Asia-Pacific Journal of Teacher Education*, 34 (1).

Murphy, J. (2005). *Connecting teacher leadership and school improvement*. Thousand Oaks, CA: Corwin Press.

Neuman, S.B. (2016). Code red: The danger of data-driven instruction. *Educational Leadership*, 74 (3), 24–29.

Papay, J.P. & Kraft, M.A. The myth of the performance plateau. *Educational Leadership*, 73 (8), 36–42.

Peske, H.G., Johnson, S.M., Kardos, S.M., Kauffman, D., & Liu, E. (2001). The next generation of teachers: Changing conceptions of a career in teaching. *Phi Delta Kappan*, 83 (4), 304–341.

Peoples, D.A. (1992). *Presentations plus: David People's proven techniques* (2nd edition). Hoboken, NJ: John Wiley & Sons Inc.

Peterson, K.D. & Deal, T.E. (2002). *The shaping school culture fieldbook*. San Francisco, CA: Jossey-Bass.

Pfeffer, J. (1992). *Managing with power: Politics and influence in organizations*. Boston, MA: Harvard Business School Press.

Phelps, P.H. (2008). Helping teachers become leaders. *The Clearing House*, 81 (3) 119–122.

Popham, J.W. (2008). All about assessment: Anchoring down the data. *Educational Leadership*, 66 (4), 85–86.

Reeves, D.B. (2008). The learning leader: Looking deeper into the data. *Educational Leadership*, 66 (4), 89–90.

Reeves, D.B. (2009). *Leading change in your school: How to conquer myths, build commitment and get results*. Alexandria, VA: Association for Supervision and Curriculum Development.

Ronfeldt, M., Loeb, S. & Wyckoff, J. (2012). *How teacher turnover harms student achievement*. Washington, DC: American Institute for Research.

Ronfeldt, M., Farmer, S.O., McQueen, K. & Grissom, J.A. (2015). Teacher collaboration in instructional teams and student achievement. *American Education Research Journal*, 52 (3).

Roulin, N. (2017). *The psychology of job interviews*. London, UK: Routledge Press.

Schein, E.H. (2004). *Organizational culture and leadership*. San Francisco, CA: Jossey-Bass.

Smith, T.M. & Ingersoll, R.M. (2004). What are the effects of induction and mentoring on beginning teacher turnover? *American Educational Research Journal*, 41 (3).

Tomal, D.R., Schilling, C.A. & Wilhite, R.K. (2014). *The teacher leader: Core competencies and strategies for effective leadership*. Lanham, MD: Rowman and Littlefield Publishing.

Watkins, M. (2003). *The first 90 days*. Boston, MA: Harvard Business School Press.

Wilson, M. (2014). Critical reflection on authentic leadership and school leader development from a virtue ethical perspective. *Educational Review*, 66 (4).

York-Barr, J. & Duke, K. (2004). What do we know about teacher leadership? Findings from two decades of scholarship. *Review of Educational Research*, 74 (3), 255–316.

# About the Author

**Matthew Jennings** has served as a public school educator for twenty-eight years. He has served as a superintendent, assistant superintendent, director of student services, supervisor of curriculum and instruction, and a classroom teacher. He earned his master's degree and doctorate in educational administration from Rutgers University.

In addition to presenting at numerous state and national conferences, Dr. Jennings has served as a consultant to school districts throughout New Jersey. He has taught as an adjunct professor for Rutgers University and the College of New Jersey. In addition to publishing books with the Association for Supervision and Curriculum Development, Corwin Press and Rowman and Littlefield, his work has been published in *Kappan, Preventing School Failure, The New Jersey English Journal, Channels, The Writing Teacher,* and the *American School Boards Journal.*

When he is not spending time with his wife MaryAnn, and his children Ryan and Tara, Dr. Jennings enjoys time at the beach, exercising and travel. He is looking forward to hiking the Appalachian Trail upon his retirement from public education.

www.ingramcontent.com/pod-product-compliance
Lightning Source LLC
Chambersburg PA
CBHW022015300426
44117CB00005B/210